American Idealism

FLOYD STOVALL

NORMAN

UNIVERSITY OF OKLAHOMA PRESS

1943

23381

To the Memory of

H. J. S.

Preface

I BELIEVE THAT DEMOCRACY will be the salvation of mankind in the coming centuries, that the philosophy of democracy is fundamentally idealistic in nature, and that it has received its fullest expression in American literature. I believe moreover that the positive faith of the American past still survives in the literature of the past, and indeed in some of the literature of the present, and I am convinced that the writers of the next generation will rediscover and reaffirm that faith. In the strength of this conviction I have set down this report of the rise and decline of idealism in American literature and have pointed out the evidences of its probable resurgence in the not distant future. I earnestly hope that those who read this essay will be encouraged to hold more firmly than ever to their American heritage of democratic idealism and to their faith in man's power eventually to build a happier and more stable world.

I acknowledge my indebtedness to the following authors and publishers for their kind permission to quote from published works: Sidney Lanier, *Poems*, edited by his wife, published by Charles Scribner's Sons, New York, 1892; William Vaughn Moody, *Poems and Plays* (2 vols.), published by Houghton Mifflin Co., 1912; Edwin

Arlington Robinson, *Collected Poems*, published by The Macmillan Co., New York, 1937; Robert Frost, *Collected Poems*, published by Henry Holt and Co., New York, 1939; Vachel Lindsay, *Collected Poems*, revised ed., published by The Macmillan Co., New York, 1925; Carl Sandburg, *Slabs of the Sunburnt West* (1922) and *The People, Yes* (1936), published by Harcourt, Brace and Co., New York; Edna St. Vincent Millay, *Make Bright the Arrows*, published by Harper & Bros., New York, 1939; Robinson Jeffers, *Selected Poems*, published by Random House, New York, 1937; Horace Gregory, *Chorus for Survival*, published by Covici Friede, Inc., New York, 1935; Willa Cather, *Death Comes for the Archbishop*, published by Alfred A. Knopf, Inc., New York, 1927; Sinclair Lewis, *Main Street* (1920), *Babbitt* (1922), and *Arrowsmith* (1925), published by Harcourt, Brace and Co., New York; John Dos Passos, *The Big Money*, published by Harcourt, Brace and Co., New York, 1936; Thomas Wolfe, *Look Homeward, Angel* (1929), *Of Time and the River* (1935), and *The Story of a Novel* (1936), published by Charles Scribner's Sons, New York; Thomas Wolfe, *You Can't Go Home Again*, published by Harper & Bros., New York, 1940; John Steinbeck, *The Grapes of Wrath*, published by The Viking Press, New York, 1939.

I am also indebted to the editors of *College English* for permission to reprint in Chapter III a substantial part of my essay "The Value of Emerson Today," which appeared in that periodical for February, 1942.

To my contemporaries and predecessors in the study of American literature and American idealism I owe much

more than I can possibly acknowledge in specific terms.
I especially thank those among my friends whose criti-
cisms have eliminated some of the many imperfections
of this work.

FLOYD STOVALL

Denton, Texas
   January 10, 1943.

The Chapters

American Idealism

I

The roots from which we spring

"IN AMERICA," FACETIOUSLY remarked George Santayana, "there is a tacit optimistic assumption about existence, to the effect that the more existence the better." It would be hard to find a better statement of the peculiar quality which distinguishes Americans as a class from other peoples. We are delighted with the geographical immensity and unparalleled wealth of our country, and swell with pride at the thought that we have more automobiles and telephones than all other nations combined. We live extensively rather than intensively, estimating the value of travel in terms of miles. The scientist's awesome revelations exhilarate us because they appeal to our sense of the terrible power and beauty of the universe. We are as large in our giving as in our having, and in our god-like generosity would embrace and nourish all humanity. Although we accept good fortune as our due, we are ready to share our benefits with all who can show themselves worthy and in need.

The typical American has more than other men the feeling of freedom and power. He believes himself invincible and immortal. He is forgetful of the past, dissatisfied with the present, and hopeful of the future. A tireless experimenter, his faith in human nature and in

the power of education is without limit. His very egotism is heartening because it is naïve, as if it were but the
measure of his pride in his humanity. Beyond question,
he is a materialist; yet in his heart of hearts he is also
a perfectionist and an idealist. He who would understand
America must resolve this contradiction.

In its origins the American nation differs from other
nations in three principal ways: first, the land on which
it was founded is continental in area and rich in natural
resources; second, it was from the beginning widely
separated, though not completely isolated, from the Old
World; and, third, its people had at the time of its settlement already reached a comparatively high level of civilization. The English settlers of Virginia and New England had just emerged from the successive waves of intellectual and spiritual advancement which we know as
the Renaissance and the Reformation. If they had not
been thus enlightened they could have made little progress against the savagery of the wilderness and might
even have adapted themselves to it. On the other hand,
if America had been more accessible to the Old World,
whatever culture it might have developed must inevitably have been absorbed by the dominant old world culture. Finally, if America had been an island instead of
a continent it would have been quickly filled and would
never have developed in its settlers that expansive imagination which has come to be characteristic of their de-
scendants.

The Renaissance and the Reformation were the culmination of a long and painful process by which a new
conception of the individual was developed that changed
his relation to society and to God. Throughout the thou-

sand years of the medieval period in Europe the individual was neglected. The system of feudal allegiances
shut him up in the small circle of his immediate community, and all his relationships with the greater world were
in the hands of the baronial overlord to whom he owed
fealty. The baron stood between the vassal and the king,
and of the three members of this group it was the vassal
who gained least. Political changes that culminated during the Renaissance so weakened the power of the barons
that they ceased to be an impassable barrier between the
individual and the king, and a new relation came into
existence to which there were only two parties, the citizen and the sovereign. Similarly, the Roman Catholic
Church stood between man and God as the medium
through which alone the two might be brought together.
The Reformation attempted to remove the Church from
this medial position and enable the individual to communicate directly with God.

These processes, which were only begun by the Renaissance and the Reformation, have never been completed in any society. Let us imagine what we may expect
to have when they are completed, supposing for the moment that they can be. With the elimination of feudal
barriers and the establishment of a direct relationship
between the king and his subjects, the subjects are reduced to an equal status and the king loses his personal
character in government and becomes the sovereign. Obviously the king does not possess sovereignty in his own
person but is only the symbol of the real sovereign, which
is the people. To be sovereign is to be absolute; hence
the people are absolute in their political power. But the
people are also, as individuals, all equal, and power is

expressed through the individual, whether the king or some other official head, who is the symbol of sovereignty. Hence it follows that each individual is sovereign in his own right, since he is equal in all respects to whatever other individual is for the time clothed with sovereignty. He cannot exercise his sovereignty freely if it conflicts with other sovereignties, and thence arises the necessity of co-operation. His sovereignty is not impaired by co-operation because it is a voluntary waiver of individual rights for the advantage of the whole community. This is the theory of democracy.

Analogous changes occur in the realm of the spirit. When the Church ceases to be the necessary mediator between the individual soul and God, the ministers of the Church lose their special character, and all men stand equal before God, their spiritual sovereign. Thus we have on the one hand God, and on the other hand a community of souls, whose spiritual life is an expression of the will of God even as the political life of a people is the expression of its sovereign. But the spiritual life issues from the people themselves, and not from without; hence God tends to lose his personal character and become a symbol of that sovereign spiritual power which is universal and absolute, and which finds its expression through the individual soul. But the individual cannot know the universal except in a mystical union in which he is identified with the object of his knowledge. It follows, therefore, that the individual, in the moment of intuitive knowledge, is identical with God and absolute in his own right. This is the doctrine of transcendentalism.

I have over-simplified the process of democratization in politics and in religion in order to make clear the principle involved. Such an absolute democracy as I have described may prove to be impossible of attainment, but it is useful as an ideal to aim at. Once establish direct communication between the individual citizen and the sovereign and the way is open for the evolution of the democratic state. The process has gone far already; how much farther it can go I shall not presume to conjecture. At best the way will be, as it has been, long and violent. It will perhaps be shorter and less violent if it is paralleled by the analogous evolution in the relationship of the individual soul and God as I have outlined it in the preceding paragraph. The essential condition is that sovereignty inhere in the individual and that all individuals be equal. A society is democratic in the degree to which it approaches this ideal.

Any attempt to trace the mystical concept of the individual to its origins would lead us through the mazes of medieval dialectics at least as far as Augustine. Such an attempt would certainly prove unprofitable. For the purposes of this study it will suffice to begin with Puritanism in New England in the seventeenth century. The orthodox theology of Puritanism was Calvinistic, but there were many heresies abroad and some differences of interpretation even among the orthodox. All agreed, however, that nothing must come between the soul and its Creator, except, of course, the Bible, which was not an obstacle but the revealed will of God. Calvin conceived of God in terms of the Old Testament, and so made him something of an oriental potentate. Sovereignty, he believed, inheres in the personal will of God, and man is powerless and insignificant before him. God exists apart from the universe he created, though he governs it in the minutest detail through his personal will, and in his essence he is unknowable. Through Adam's transgression and fall, all men are born depraved and sinning creatures, but God has extended grace to a few, who are elected from the beginning to be saved; all the rest are denied grace and must therefore suffer damnation and eternal punishment for their sins.

Reduced to its simplest terms, the problem of New England Puritanism was to reconcile the dogma of predestination with the human experience of morality. Orthodox thinkers taught that man's will is not free except in the limited sphere of God's allowance. They found it expedient, however, to insist that God holds man morally accountable for his actions. To reconcile these contradictions they developed their doctrine of grace. Calvin had taught that God's will is arbitrary and that his willing an action made it a moral action. He extended grace to certain individuals, not because they deserved it, but for reasons that lie beyond human understanding. As a consequence of receiving grace, these individuals were regenerated and became moral agents. Thus Calvinism opposed the Roman Catholic doctrine that God gives grace as a reward for good works. The Puritan divines, though hating the Catholic doctrine of salvation through good works, nevertheless felt that it would be unreasonable for God to save a man and yet withhold from him the assurance of salvation. They argued that a regenerated man would feel inclined to works of piety, and would know because of this inclination that he was regenerated. Such a doctrine was politically useful too, since only the regenerated could vote, and it was necessary to have some objective evidence of regeneration.

The effect of this doctrine was to support the high moral tone of Puritan society, which is perhaps its most admirable feature. Yet this doctrine of morality as an effect of grace was delicately balanced between a too enthusiastic acceptance of grace on the one hand and a too skeptical rationalism on the other. New England thinkers were, in general, divided into three groups: the Antinomians, including all those who interpreted grace as a mystical union with Christ; the Arminians, including all those, however differing in other matters, who believed that man is free to accept or reject God's grace when it is offered and even to earn it as a reward for good deeds; and the orthodox, who devised the Covenant of Grace as a compromise between these two extremes.

The most famous of the Antinomians was Mistress Anne Hutchinson, who was brought to trial in Boston in 1637, condemned because she declared that God had made known his truths to her, as to Abraham, by a special revelation, and banished to Rhode Island, where she was killed in an Indian massacre four years later. The saints of Massachusetts perceived in her death a judgment from heaven. Before her fall Mrs. Hutchinson's influence had been sufficient to draw the allegiance of John Cotton and Sir Harry Vane, who was governor for a year. It is possible that the majority of the inhabitants of Boston were on her side, but of course the most powerful group, including all of the orthodox ministers, were against her.

It was probably not Mrs. Hutchinson's intention to disturb the practice of morality in New England, but if, as she taught, the regenerated and sanctified person took on the perfection of Christ and became a law unto himself, it would obviously be difficult to bind him to any objective code of ethics. Undoubtedly such a doctrine is dangerous, but New England was, as we shall presently see, not to be rid of it by the expedient of banishment.

Other unorthodox ideas suspiciously close to Antinomianism were taught by Anabaptists, Seekers, and Quakers. These groups were not as dangerous as Mrs. Hutchinson's party because they were composed mostly of poor and uneducated persons. All of them were persecuted and harried out of Massachusetts because they encouraged the individual to despise authority and live according to the promptings of the heart, the "inner light" of the Quakers. Sooner or later they found their way to Rhode Island, where, under the leadership of Roger Williams, free thinkers of all kinds were slowly and with some confusion laying the foundations for democratic society.

Although the defenders of orthodoxy did not realize it at first, the Arminians were more to be feared than the Antinomians because their poison was more subtle and because the infection quickly spread through the camp of the faithful. Antinomianism and Arminianism were the two poles of Puritanism, the former tending to an unreasoning piety and the other to a purely ethical rationalism. Antinomianism led to mysticism and evangelism, whereas Arminianism led to deism and Unitarianism. The orthodox took the view that Puritanism was the synthesis of piety and reason, but in practice they came more and more to emphasize reason at the expense of piety. This was inevitable, since the undisciplined enthusiasts proved to be a greater menace to the moral stability of their social order than the intellectual humanists; moreover, they could banish the former, but hardly the latter.

To embody their understanding of the synthesis of piety and reason the Puritans formulated the Covenant of Grace. There had been an original Covenant of Works between God and Adam, whereby God promised to Adam and his posterity eternal life if he would do certain things. Adam failed, and as a consequence his posterity lost the privilege of winning God's favor by good works. They too had, in Adam's sin, broken the Covenant. But God made a new Covenant with Abraham whereby God, in the person of Christ, takes upon himself the penalty of the broken Covenant of Works and requires of man not works but faith. They who believe in Christ as the Redeemer will have Christ's righteousness ascribed to them, will be therefore justified, and so capable of performing the works required in the moral law. If man will believe, God is bound to restore him to the place in the original covenant which was lost through Adam. This does not impair God's sovereignty because God willingly limits himself by the terms of the Covenant of Grace. When a man is converted he becomes a party to the Covenant of Grace and also assumes the obligation to fulfill the Covenant of Works.

Professor Perry Miller, in his valuable study *The New England Mind,* calls the Covenant of Grace a "legalized version of Biblical history." It enabled the Puritans to make man responsible to the moral law, but it also assured him that he would be duly rewarded for his good works. By its means the Puritans escaped, or thought they escaped, from the paralyzing effect of determinism and acquired freedom of will within a prescribed area. One suspects that it was also a scheme to guarantee a profit to the investor in virtue. In any case it was a long step away from Calvinism in the direction of Unitarianism, and I think we may credit the change largely to the influence of Arminianism.

But before New England abandoned Calvinism it was to have one last champion, the most brilliant of them all, in Jonathan Edwards. His writings appeared in the second third of the eighteenth century, at a time when the theology of Calvin was going through its death struggles. He was a man of sensitive feeling and imagination, a keen logician, and a masterful stylist. He believed that religious experience was a matter of the affections more than of the reason, though the reason too must be satisfied. In his *Personal Narrative* he tells how, from childhood on, he had found objections to the doctrine of God's sovereignty in choosing whom he pleased for eternal life and rejecting whom he pleased. And he could not tell how or by what means he was finally convinced, realizing only that his reason apprehended the justice of it. He became a close student of Hobbes, Locke, and other philosophers whose works were influential at that time, but he was also a preacher of great emotional power. His emotionalism is illustrated in the following passage from his *Personal Narrative*, describing an experience of grace and a vision of Christ:

The person of Christ appeared ineffably excellent with an excellency great enough to swallow up all thought and conception—which continued as near as I can judge, about an hour; which kept me the greater part of the time in a flood of tears, and weeping aloud. I felt an ardency of soul to be, what I know not otherwise how to express, emptied and annihilated; to lie in the dust, and to be full of Christ alone; to love him with a holy and pure love; to trust in him; to live upon him; to serve and follow him; and to be perfectly sanctified and made pure, with a divine and heavenly purity.

This annihilation of self in an emotional and mystical union with Christ is both a survival of the pietism of the seventeenth century and an example of the new emotionalism in evangelistic religion which began with the Great Awakening and has continued in one form or another to the present time.

In his later years Edwards dedicated himself to the task of proving God's sovereignty by logical demonstration. In his famous treatise on *Freedom of the Will*, he argued that a volition, which is an act of the will, must, like any other event, have a cause. Volitional impulses spring from motives, and motives are determined by desires. The will, therefore, is wholly passive, being determined by something outside itself. He defines liberty as the power or opportunity a man has to do as he desires. The desire itself is not subject to his will, but is determined. He accepted the Calvinistic doctrine that man, because of Adam's sin, is totally depraved and unable to feel anything except selfish desires. Yet he defined virtue as disinterested benevolence. Obviously man has no power in himself to become virtuous, and he may become so only if God's "efficacious, determining grace" changes him completely and endues him with benevolence. Conversion is the participation in the divine nature whereby the soul acquires a supernatural sense and images the glory that it beholds.

In spite of his rationalism, Edwards remained essentially a Puritan mystic. Union with God was a transient experience involving the annihilation, not the expansion, of the self; and when the experience of grace was past, the rational faculty reasserted itself. Hence in all practical affairs he was guided by reason, not by intuition, which he took to be an experience of emotion rather than of mind.

Edwards said that God, in the person of Christ, created the world to the end that he might "communicate Himself in an image of His own excellency." Each thing images God's excellency according to its capacity. Spirits, which are real beings, have the capacity to image God more perfectly than bodies, which are but the shadows of real beings. Man, through the fall, lost his capacity to image God perfectly, but will receive it back in heaven. Nature retains its original capacity unimpaired by the fall of man, because the beauty of nature is an immediate emanation of the beauty of God. Hence the beauty of nature, though imperfect, is for the mind of man a suggestive image of divine beauty.

This concept of nature is thoroughly in keeping with Puritan theology and is not to be confused with Emerson's concept of nature as the incarnation of God in the unconscious state. The two concepts have enough in common, nevertheless, to remind us that Emerson's philosophy was not altogether antithetical to Puritanism but, in part at least, a development from it. Their views on man differ more widely. Whereas Edwards believed man lost, with Adam's fall, his capacity to image the excellency of God, Emerson believed that he retained it, at least potentially.

The evangelism of Jonathan Edwards was the most influential element in his life's work; his rather cautious mysticism, finding the temper of the age uncongenial, had little effect. It was an anomaly in the Calvinistic tradition. Mysticism survived in New England, where it survived at all, most effectually among the Quakers. But the Quakers were not welcome there, except in Rhode Island, and we must look elsewhere among the colonies for the fullest development of their philosophy.

Conditions were most favorable for the Society of Friends in the middle colonies, particularly New Jersey and Pennsylvania. The personal and political influence of William Penn made possible the establishment of a Quaker colony in Pennsylvania, where the Friends were allowed to exemplify their philosophy of pacifism and quietism undisturbed until the latter half of the eighteenth century, when they sacrificed their political power rather than take part in the wars of that period.

For the purposes of the present study, not William Penn but John Woolman was the most important of the Quakers. For their illumination the Quakers looked neither to an authoritarian doctrine nor the human reason, but to a personal revelation, an "inner light," which God imparts to each individual. As Woolman says, "It is deep and inward, confined to no forms of religion, nor excluded from any, when the heart stands in perfect sincerity." And they in whose hearts this divine principle takes root become brethren. John Woolman was a citizen of New Jersey, a simple man, whose title to fame lies not in the formulation of a creed or philosophy, but in the exemplification of the noblest qualities of Christian idealism. In his diary, which was published in 1774, appear the full beauty and dignity of the Quaker faith in the inward life and the Quaker ideal of self-denial and charity towards all men.

A generation or more after Woolman, Elias Hicks became the leader of a faction among the Quakers who denied the supernatural character of Christ and affirmed that it was not the material blood of Jesus that saved but the immaterial blood of his soul. "The soul of man has no material blood," said Elias Hicks; "but as the outward material blood, created from the dust of the earth, is the life of these bodies of flesh, so with respect to the soul, the immortal and invisible spirit, its blood is that life which God breathed into it." Unquestionably, Hicks had gone far beyond the doctrine allowed by orthodox Quakers and had taken a position very near to transcendentalism. It is not without significance that Walt Whitman's father and mother took him to hear the old Quaker preach when Walt was a boy of ten, and that he became himself an expounder of many of the principles of the Quakers.

But mysticism had little encouragement in America between 1750 and 1820. Deism was at once more vigorous and more practical, and it spread rapidly from England and France through the eastern sections of the American colonies during the first half of this period. In fact it had been threatening to invade the ranks of the Puritans for half a century before that, as we have seen. Deists contended that God exists wholly outside and apart from the physical universe, of which man is a part, and that his action upon this universe is altogether impersonal and mechanical. It was a purely rationalistic philosophy, leaving no place for the emotional, the mystical, or the supernatural experience. Its principal effect was to center man's attention upon social problems by removing God beyond the sphere of human interest. It was accompanied by, and partly responsible for, the humanitarian movement which has been such a powerful agent in the determination of social and political forms in the modern world.

I shall not attempt to give the history of deism. Its first great exponent in America was Benjamin Franklin, who has sometimes been called the first modern American. Franklin had nothing in common with Edwards and very little in common with Woolman; and yet the practical, scientific, and rational character of the American mind, so notable in the case of Franklin, was present and very active long before his time. Samuel Sewall, for example, was a sort of Calvinist Franklin, and even Cotton Mather was an amateur scientist. Besides Franklin, the best known of the deists were Ethan Allen, Thomas Paine, and Thomas Jefferson, all of whom were prominent in the dissemination of democratic ideas during the Revolution and the early national period.

The deistic movement was not in opposition to idealism. Rather it was the mind's rebellion against the anthropomorphism of the Calvinistic theology, and it was probably a necessary clearing of the ground for the rise of transcendentalism. It was akin to Calvinism in that it conceived God as outside the human world, but it was like transcendentalism in that it repudiated superstition and all supernatural effects of the supreme will.

Edwards and Franklin are said to represent two aspects of the American mind. In one aspect it seeks, like Edwards, whether intuitively or rationally, for an absolute principle that will satisfy man's desire for unity in the universe. In the other aspect it is, like Franklin, pragmatic, seizing what is available to accomplish the greatest possible immediate good for the community and the individual. Franklin is blandly human; he admits his imper-

fection, but hopes to improve. In him are united the Yankee ingenuity and the rational spirit of the eighteenth century. His Americanism, although not more genuine than
that of Edwards, is more obvious because it is extrinsic and
belongs to the experience of the community, whereas that
of Edwards is intrinsic and belongs to the experience of
the soul. Both are idealisms, but one is an idealism for the
self and the other is an idealism for society.

Deism was more, however, than rebellion against
Calvinism; it was also and beyond this an inevitable development of the rational elements which had persisted
in Protestant theology from the beginning; and it was,
finally, a product, in part, of the scientific discoveries of
Bacon and Newton and their contemporaries. Out of the
deist's concern with the order of nature arose the theory
of progress, and from his interest in social problems came
the doctrine of natural rights. I do not mean, of course,
that either of these ideas originated in the eighteenth century, but it was in that century that they became an active
force in the affairs of men. Whatever we may think now
of the philosophical validity of these ideas, there can be
no question of the fact that they were powerful agents in
precipitating the French and American revolutions and in
shaping the political structure of our nation.

But what became of the Calvinistic ministers in a
deistic world? In the main they continued to perform their
functions as before, with perhaps less brimstone in their
sermons. But some of them deserted the old beliefs altogether and became Unitarians. There was, in fact, a definite kinship between deism and Unitarianism. Both were
products of the rational mind, both denied the mystery of
the Trinity, reducing Christ to the status of a superior

man, and both affirmed their belief in the irresistible progress of man towards perfection. Neither deism nor Unitarianism has been popular in religious groups in the United States, and deism particularly has been fiercely attacked by the orthodox of most churches as a teaching of infidelity. Thomas Paine, although no worse than other deists, has been set up as the very image of Satan. Thomas Jefferson has been spared because his deistic writings are not well known and because he has been a popular hero on other grounds.Unitarianism has appealed chiefly to those in whom the intellect is a more active force than the emotions, and especially to the intellectual classes in the neighborhood of Boston in the early decades of the nineteenth century. The most famous of the Unitarian preachers and thinkers was William Ellery Channing, who taught that human nature is essentially good, that salvation is by character and not by grace, and that unlimited progress is possible both for the individual and for society.

Such concepts as freedom, equality, progress, and natural rights were readily accepted as true of the frontier, where life was reduced to its simplest terms of man in conflict with the forces of nature. In this elemental struggle the nonessentials of formal society were soon dropped. If the process had not involved more than this sloughing-off of the polite acquirements of society the frontiersman would simply have reverted to savagery. But it did involve more; for the frontiersman was not permanently cut off from civilization, and when he did return to it, or when eventually it came to him, he was in a position to choose consciously what he would keep and what he would reject. In short, he was permitted to create a new culture from the adaptation of the old ideas to the new physical conditions of the frontier. It was the dream of men in all ages: the dream of beginning over, of a second chance, a new life with the benefit of old experience. It was the story of Robinson Crusoe on a continental scale.

It must not be supposed that this new world was immediately better than the old. It brought many new evils, and it soon revived many of the evils from which it had at first been a refuge. The frontiersmen were not possessed of the most advanced ideas, and by the time these ideas arrived at a new community, other ideas less advanced had got a strong foothold. Hence the worst features of Calvinistic theology were perpetuated on the frontier long after they had been discarded in the East. Such ideas, however, as freedom, equality, and natural rights flourished on the frontier and from there pushed back eastward, not as ideas but as action. Indeed this was the most effective contribution of the frontier, that it translated old ideas into action that changed the course of our development as it could not have been changed, probably, if the ideas had remained subject to the traditions and established prejudices of the Old World. The real America is therefore not to be found either in the order of the long-settled communities or in the disorder of the frontier, but in that area of dynamic and expanding life which is born of the union of the two.

This union of West and East, of the frontier spirit with the intellectual heritage of the past, was best exemplified in the mind and character of Thomas Jefferson. The ideals of individualism and democracy had developed, through many vicissitudes, from the premature efforts of Roger Williams to fruition in the Revolution, and to classic expression in the Declaration of Independence. But they might have been lost in the federalist and monarchist reaction that followed had it not been for the fortunate conjunction of the French Revolution, with its slogan of liberty, equality, and fraternity, and the dynamic personalities of Thomas Paine and Thomas Jefferson. Paine's *Rights of Man* and other stirring pamphlets had great influence at the time, but Paine did not long remain in this country, and without Jefferson his work might have proved ineffectual. Because Jefferson was twice president of the United States and because he was the founder of a lasting political philosophy, his ideals were firmly established in the national consciousness. It is doubtful whether these ideals could have become a force in world affairs, however, if they had not been caught up by the expansive enthusiasm of the frontier and carried, with the American flag, across the continent.

These, then, compose the foundations of American idealism, the roots from which we spring: the mysticism and moral power inherent in Puritanism, the rational liberalism and faith in human nature that developed in the thought of the eighteenth century, and the expansive spirit of the frontier, which gives to the whole its peculiarly American character. How American idealism, thus based, has grown to a full body of democratic faith, how it declined after the Civil War, and to what extent it still survives I shall attempt to describe in the succeeding chapters of this work.

II

Early Writers

FROM THE PRECEDING CHAPTER it may be seen that the foundations of American idealism were laid in the forms of religion and politics. In the Old World as well as in the New, people's minds were pre-occupied during the seventeenth century with the struggle for religious freedom, and during the eighteenth with the struggle for political freedom. By the end of the latter, both struggles had been won by the American settlers. This was fortunate, because these two freedoms are the necessary conditions to all other freedoms and must be established before the superstructure of a democratic society can be safely erected.

I say that religious and political freedom had been won, but that is not altogether true. With the adoption by the several states of the Federal Constitution and the ten amendments known as the Bill of Rights, every individual in the United States became possessed of the legal right to worship as he pleased. Intolerance was not abolished, however, and indeed cannot be abolished by legislative enactments. Similarly, the political freedom of the citizen, although it is now guaranteed by the constitution and its amendments, is limited by the inability of the individual to form independent judgments. In the last analysis the case for freedom in a democracy rests with the individual. He must be intellectually qualified to have opinions; but intellect in itself is not enough; we of the twentieth century have been taught both by experience and the authority of science that our opinions, far more often than our fathers had supposed, have their origin in the emotions. In a democracy, therefore, both the intellect and the emotions must be cultivated if freedom is to be preserved.

Granting that freedom is attained or attainable, what then? What is it that we have freedom to do or to be? For freedom is not an end in itself but the means to an end, the opportunity to disintegrate or to grow. It may be assumed that neither the individual nor organized society desires its own undoing; the will to live is the will to grow, and the will to grow implies something to grow to. Thus it is that as individuals and as societies we have purposes, though we do not always formulate them, and we have ideals, though we do not always define them. Since an ideal is something yet unrealized it cannot be wholly known or clearly defined; it exists more effectively in the realm of feeling than in the realm of thought, and it yields more to the imagination of the artist than to the intellect of the scientist.

Idealism is a vague term, and doubtless much abused. We speak of it in connection with politics, business, religion, and education as if it were in itself a mere abstraction. In philosophy, even, the word tends to collect adjectives, such as objective, subjective, rational, and so on. But there is one thing common to all idealisms, namely, the belief that the way of life is not a blind alley, that behind universal change lies purpose, and that purpose is an expression of mind. It is sometimes hard to distinguish an idealist from a realist or even, now that impenetrable matter has been dissolved in the laboratory, from a materialist, but he has no affinity with the defeatists. He has faith in man as a spiritual being endowed by nature or else by a supernatural Creator with the power to conceive objective values, which he calls the good, the true, and the beautiful, and the effective will to attain them.

I shall not attempt to trace the history of idealism in American philosophical thought. Indeed, America can hardly be said to have produced philosophers, as distinguished from theologians, political thinkers, and literary men, until the last quarter of the nineteenth century. Having at last arrived, the philosophers discovered that science had become the dominant force in American intellectual life, and they were driven, for lack of a wider audience, to write for one another; as a consequence, their language became more and more esoteric and incomprehensible to the untrained reader. It devolved, therefore, upon men of letters to perform the function in the nineteenth century which in the seventeenth and eighteenth had been performed by theologians and political thinkers. Especially has literature been the medium for the dissemination of those ideas and beliefs which constitute the body of American idealism. If these ideas and beliefs are to be preserved for our democratic society, to sustain it and to revive it, they are most likely to be preserved in our literature.

There is no American literature, strictly speaking, of the seventeenth century. All except a few who were writing at that time had been born in England, and most of what they wrote was theological in content and didactic in purpose. In moral force and intellectual power these pioneers were richly endowed, but the austerity of their religion and the physical hardships they endured were not conducive to the development of the sentiments and the imagination, which are so essential to the production of literary art.

Of their prose I need add nothing to what I have already said in my first chapter. They were prolific in verse as in prose, most of the verses being composed by ministers in commemoration or praise of other ministers. There were two poets: Mrs. Anne Bradstreet and Michael Wigglesworth. The latter was a minister who preached sermons in doggerel but was otherwise not different from his fellow ministers, and therefore we need not concern ourselves further with him. Mrs. Bradstreet's case is somewhat different. That she should have written at all is unusual considering the prejudices of her time, but that she should have written so well and so much, though the mother of eight children in a pioneer community, is evidence of remarkable qualities of mind and character. There must have been other women, her neighbors, with like qualities but without her gift of expression. In her poems, and also in her letters, we see the tender and more gracious side of Puritanism as well as the piety. Here was one who loved nature both for its beauty and as a symbol of God's creative will. She was the spiritual mother of Emerson no less than of Edwards. It is interesting, and perhaps significant, that the first poet in America was a woman and one so rich in the virtues peculiar to her sex.

The period from about 1675 to 1725 was the most sterile in the history of New England. Then lived the second and third generations of Puritans, after John Cotton and Roger Williams and before Jonathan Edwards, the generations of Increase and Cotton Mather. Not until the last quarter of the eighteenth century was there any genuine literary activity, unless the writings of Edwards may be called literary. In 1723 the boy Franklin, feeling the frigidity of the intellectual atmosphere, removed to Philadelphia. His *Autobiography*, which is his principal claim to literary fame, was not written until well past the middle of the century. Somewhat earlier the aristocratic planter, William Byrd, of Virginia, was describing in his polished and charmingly humorous prose the life of the American frontier as he saw it along the boundary line of Virginia and North Carolina. He presented the freedom and individualism of the frontiersmen in the worst possible light, and yet the discerning reader may, in spite of the ridicule of the author, perceive some of the forces that produced Jacksonian democracy.

In the last quarter of the century, stimulated by the American Revolution, several writers conceived and executed ambitious literary projects. Three of these were Connecticut men, graduates of Yale College, who came to maturity about the beginning of the Revolution. The oldest, John Trumbull, was a rather clever satirist in verse and used his talents effectively for independence; however, he turned to law afterwards and grew increasingly conservative, identifying himself finally with the Federalist Party. Next in age to Trumbull was Timothy Dwight, who, as befitted the grandson of Jonathan Edwards, devoted his pen to the destruction of deism and the revival of Calvinism, but with indifferent success. He became president of Yale and a staunch Federalist. These two poets were useful citizens, but they contributed little to the advance of liberal ideas. Joel Barlow, author of the patriotic but heavy epic *The Columbiad*, was the third and youngest of this group of Connecticut poets. Unlike the other two, he became more liberal as he grew older, possibly because he resided for a number of years in revolutionary France. Like his friend Tom Paine, he wrote a reply to Burke's *Reflections on the French Revolution*. Barlow defended the Revolution and argued that republican government is "the only government proper to ensure the happiness and support the dignity of man." His prose is now almost forgotten, however, and his poems are read by few except students of the history of American literature. Thus, although he was an important force in the advance of liberalism, and although the results of his work abide, the work itself seems destined to sink into oblivion.

Most gifted of the poets of the Revolution and the only one whose work is likely to survive, was Philip Freneau, of New York, poet, journalist, and sailor, friend of Jefferson, scourge of Tories, and champion of democracy. Like Barlow he was an admirer of Paine and wrote a eulogy of *The Rights of Man* in verse. He was a man of versatile talents and contradictory temper, turning from classical to romantic themes or from satiric to sentimental moods with the greatest of ease. If he is to be classified at all he belongs with Young, Collins, and Gray in the transitional era between the neo-classical and the romantic periods in English and American literature.

Freneau is the only American poet of the eighteenth century whose work reflects the romantic spirit. Thoroughly deistic in his opinions, he believed that man is naturally good and perfectible but has been corrupted and alienated from nature by the very institutions he himself has created. He was convinced, however, that man can re-

store himself to full harmony with the laws of nature by
the infallible power of reason. It is this aspect of his work,
rather than his love of Gothic horrors and romantic melancholy, that leads most directly to his democratic faith in
human nature. During the strenuous years following the
adoption of the Federal Constitution, he was editor of the
National Gazette in Philadelphia, which supported Jefferson's views, and was credited by Jefferson with saving
the country from an alarming drift towards monarchy.
He was also one of the most ardent supporters of the
French Revolution, calling upon France to continue the
struggle

> *Till Reason's laws restore*
> *Man to be Man, in every clime;—*
> *That Being, active, great, sublime,*
> *Debased in dust no more.*

In the field of fiction and the drama, talent was just
beginning to appear at the end of the eighteenth century.
Royal Tyler's *The Contrast* was in the style of Sheridan's
comedies, and William Dunlap's *André*, a historical
drama, develops a patriotic theme but is weak in plot and
characterization. It is not surprising that this country was
slow in the development of the drama, for life here lacked
the social concentration and intensity necessary to its existence. Fiction, as represented in the romances of Charles
Brockden Brown in the last decade of the century, was
somewhat more promising. Brown's fiction was in the
Gothic style of Mrs. Radcliffe and William Godwin, who
concocted a plot of strange and terrible happenings puz-
zling to the reader, but rationally explained by the author
in the conclusion. Brown's purpose, in so far as he had a

purpose aside from entertainment, was, like Godwin's, to attack superstition and to enlarge human rights, and, in addition, to point the way to the making of a distinctly American literature.

It can hardly be said that America had a literature of its own in the eighteenth century, but with the appearance of Washington Irving's first publications, the *Salmagundi* papers (1807–08) and the *Knickerbocker's History of New York* (1809), a new and brilliant era began. Although Irving was, in these early works, as much a part of the eighteenth century as either Freneau or Brockden Brown, he eschewed both deism and Gothic horror, and he subordinated the rational spirit to the spirit of wit and good-humored satire. In short, he passed entirely over the latter half of the eighteenth century and recaptured the polish and sparkle of the Augustan Age in English letters. Although *Salmagundi* and the *History* are bantering in their tone and appear to make fun of all the hallowed traditions of Americans and of New Yorkers in particular, they betray, or so it seems, a love of those same traditions that is but half concealed.

Irving's literary mind lay fallow for nearly ten years after *Knickerbocker's History,* but in the dozen years following that interval he produced eight books, including *The Sketch Book* (1819–20), *Bracebridge Hall* (1822), *Tales of a Traveller* (1824), and *The Alhambra* (1832), which were probably his four best books. With *The Sketch Book* begins his work in the romantic manner, adding a new richness and color without detracting from the Augustan purity of his style. He owed much to Scott, but the charm of his manner was quite his own. Whatever passed under the magic of his pen took on the glow and quietness of an autumn landscape and gave forth the mellow tones of distant church bells. He says of himself that he loves "the sublime and beautiful" in the natural scenery of America, but he also loves the "accumulated treasures" of Europe and "longed to tread, as it were, in the footsteps of antiquity." No one can read much of Irving without being impressed with the justness of this statement of his two romantic passions, nature and the past. He dwelt with evident pleasure upon the silent and majestic solitudes of mountains not too far removed from the city. Amidst the comfort and culture of modern civilization he liked to look back with sentimental nostalgia upon the heroic past. The country customs surviving from seventeenth-century England were more to his taste than the commonplaces of his own time, whether they were the fashions of formalized European society or the crudities of equalitarian America. Always he preferred sentiment above science, the quaint above the modern.

There was nothing of the Puritan in Irving, and very little of the democrat. He satirized the New England Puritan, somewhat decayed and turned Yankee democrat, in Ichabod Crane. He was the "conscientious" sort, smug, vain, ingratiating, and superstitious—"an odd mixture of small shrewdness and simple credulity," with an enlarged bump of acquisitiveness. Irving obviously enjoyed the caricature. And yet, after seventeen years in Europe, he returned to America surfeited with the romance of the past and ready to look for romance in the present. Soon after his arrival in America he set out in the company of government commissioners on a tour into the Southwest which led him to the Indian country in what is now eastern Oklahoma. The literary result of this experience was *A*

Tour on the Prairies. Perhaps his acquaintance with western America enabled him to perceive more clearly than before the virtues of democracy; for, although it would not be correct to say that he ever fully accepted the democratic philosophy, it is true that he learned gradually to appreciate its practical value and to make a fairly comfortable place for himself in the America of Andrew Jackson. He was so far acceptable to the Democratic Party that he was offered nominations to Congress and to the office of Mayor of New York, both of which he declined. To assure posterity of the genuineness of his Americanism he undertook and brought to completion shortly before his death a monumental biography of George Washington.

Within a very few years after Irving's success with *The Sketch Book*, James Fenimore Cooper also won acclaim with *The Spy* (1821), *The Pioneers* (1823), and other popular novels on American themes. Cooper grew up in central New York, where his father owned extensive lands, in the first generation after the pioneers in this region. The Indians had already departed for less settled country, but the wilderness remained almost untouched by civilization, and many were still living there who could remember wilder times. Thus his situation was ideal for the cultivation of the creative imagination; he was sufficiently removed from the frontier to see it through a romantically colored lens, yet close enough to know it as a stirring reality. It is not surprising that, having discovered his talent for narrative writing, he should have drawn upon this rich background of mingled fact and legend for literary treatment. The final result was the writing of five narratives, known as the "Leatherstocking Tales," woven about the adventures of an eighteenth century hunter and scout called at different times Deerslayer, Hawkeye, Pathfinder, and Leatherstocking.

Without undertaking an analysis of all or any of these romances, I would point out some of the specific qualities of this popular hero. In the gaunt figure, practical skill, and homely philosophy of Leatherstocking, Cooper has given us the type of the frontiersman. This remarkable man has all, or nearly all, of the virtues of the Indians, and in addition, many virtues of civilized men—but not too many, because much of his charm is due to his picturesque rôle as a link between the savage and the Europeanized white man. Through him Cooper shows us what the frontier, with its simplicity and its cruelty, contributed to American culture. Leatherstocking is superior both to the Indian and to the civilized white, and so stands as a kind of rustic ideal of American character. There is a good deal of the Puritan in this moralizing woodsman, and there is much of the Quaker also. He was no hand to pray or to affect piety, but he was conscious of a benign presence overflowing the face of nature. Religion was not in him a state of mind but a state of being, and he was as completely unconscious of it as he was of the beating of his heart. Yet he could not forget that he was a Christian, and when at last he lay dying on the western prairies that he never loved, he would make no un-Christian boast of valiant deeds, nor would he allow an un-Christian burial, even to gratify the pride of his adopted Indian son, of whom he was very fond.

Cooper's first book had been a novel of manners, and though it was not successful, it indicated an interest in social problems to which he later returned with more success. Always, even in his romances, he was motivated by moral rather than by æsthetic purposes; he idealized the Indian by endowing him with the moral virtues of white men and Christians. He held strong opinions on many controversial subjects, particularly the manners proper to Americans, and these drew criticism, which provoked him to more vehement opinions still, so that in the end he was involved in bickerings and libel suits that cost him much of his former popularity.

Although he was a product of the frontier, at least in part, Cooper was not a frontiersman. He spent several years in Europe, after his first successes, and though he did not adapt himself to European culture as thoroughly as Irving did, the experience gave him perspective by which he could see the faults as well as the virtues of American democracy. Besides, he was bred to wealth, married into one of the aristocratic old Dutch families of New York, and quite naturally looked with distaste upon the crudities of less refined persons. He called himself a democrat, but he was not an equalitarian. He conceded to all men equally the right to seek wealth, political preferment, and social refinement, but he denied that all men are equal in their attainment of these values, or that they ever in fact can be. An indispensable right of the individual in a democratic society, as he conceived it, is the right to be different from the rest and set his own standard of social refinement so long as he does not interfere with the rights of others. Like Carlyle and Ruskin, he was an "ethical idealist," but he had little in common with either the Puritan or the deist. His religious affinities were with the more formal and conservative churches, and in his old age he became a member of the Episcopal Church. In his politics only was he a democrat, being in his economic sympathies an agrarian and in his intellectual and social tastes an aristocrat.

Both Irving and Cooper were transitional figures, but they were imperfect representatives of the two periods that were linked together by their lives and work. William Cullen Bryant, on the other hand, was not only a link between the eighteenth and nineteenth centuries, but a remarkably perfect representative of the American spirit through all stages of its development. Born in western Massachusetts in 1794, his long life extended into the last quarter of the nineteenth century, and through his fifty years' work as editor of a large New York newspaper, he was intimately acquainted with the political, economic, and intellectual history of the nation during the era of its greatest expansion.

The influences that shaped Bryant's religious beliefs in his childhood and youth were dominantly Calvinistic, and in spite of all later influences, he never wholly escaped from the austere spirit of his early environment. As he grew up from boyhood and came to be more intimate with his father, a physician, whose ideas were more liberal than those of his mother's family, he imbibed something of the deistic freedom of thought. While in Williams College he felt the full force of the deistic movement, then strong in the colleges, and probably thought of himself for a time as a deist. Before he was twenty-five, however, he had settled into beliefs more nearly Unitarian than deistic, although he did not, at that time, become a member of the church. His views on religious matters did not change much as he grew old, but he did appear, as I have said, to revert in some measure to the spirit, not the dogmas, of Calvinism.

In politics he began as a Federalist, his first ambitious poem, *The Embargo*, written at the age of thirteen, being a satire upon President Jefferson and Jeffersonian democracy. Partly, perhaps, from his study of deistic literature, and partly from practical experiences as a lawyer in a small town, he gradually moved away from Federalist principles towards democratic ideas of human liberty, nationalism, and free trade. With a romantic idealization of frontiersmen, he championed Andrew Jackson during his campaign for the presidency, and supported him with the full power of his newspaper during his two administrations. Yet he held principle above all else, and would not support Harrison because he thought his campaign fraudulent, and opposed Tilden, a personal friend, because he considered the Democratic Party no longer truly democratic. He broke with the regular branch of the Democratic Party in 1848, joined the Free-Soil Party a little later, and eventually followed Lincoln into the new Republican Party. However, he remained an advocate of free trade to the end of his life. His faith in human nature made him an ardent individualist, in spite of all Calvinistic qualms, and his altruistic desire to make all men free and prosperous made him a democrat.

In literary theory and practice he began as a neo-classicist, writing *The Embargo* and other early poems in heroic couplets, in imitation of Pope, his father's favorite poet. Before he was sixteen, the age at which he wrote the first draft of "Thanatopsis," he had become a full-fledged romanticist, a nature-worshipper, and a blank verse poet of death. This was the romanticism of Blair, Cowper, and their contemporaries rather than the romanticism of Wordsworth and the nineteenth century, but it was only

two or three years later that Bryant felt the full force of
Wordsworth's influence. In several of his poems, and particularly in "A Forest Hymn" (1825), perhaps his finest
poem, he seems on the point of asserting Wordsworth's
mystic faith in the unity of man and nature, but he draws
back, as if afraid of the thought, and reiterates the dogma
of sinning man seeking evidence of God's grace in a sinless
nature. One may say that Bryant followed the course of
American spiritual evolution to the verge of transcendentalism but would not go all the way. His roots were too
deeply planted in the eighteenth century to permit so
complete a change; that must be the work of younger and
more daring spirits.

From Anne Bradstreet to William Cullen Bryant is a
span of nearly two hundred years, embracing two-thirds
of the life of the American people, and yet in perspective
it seems but a little while. That is due to the dominance
of Puritanism in American thought, not only in New
England but throughout the country; for though Calvinism gave way along the Atlantic coast before deism and
humanism, it remained strong among the Scotch-Irish
pioneers in the West, and was revived by a kind of meta-
morphosis in New England transcendentalism. In this
evolutionary change Calvinism, the thesis, moves outward
into deism, the antithesis, which then returns to fuse with
Calvinism and transform it into transcendentalism, the
synthesis. By the end of the second century after the land-
ing of the Pilgrims, the first full cycle of American intellectual development was completed and the time was
ripe, in New England at least, for the philosophical formulation of American idealism. This was to be the work
of Emerson.

III

Emerson

R ALPH WALDO EMERSON
was wholly of New England and the nineteenth century,
having been born in Boston, May 25, 1803, of a long line
of Puritans, many of them ministers. His religious experience began where Bryant's ended, in Unitarianism.
His father, William Emerson, pastor of the First Church,
was a man of liberal views who loved life and literature. At the time Emerson was an undergraduate at Harvard, Dr. William Ellery Channing, the great Unitarian preacher and critic, was in his prime and exercised a
strong influence upon the minds of young intellectuals. It
is natural, therefore, that young Emerson, following the
traditions of his family, should enter the ministry. He became pastor of the Second Church in Boston; but already
he had outgrown Unitarianism, and finding his office con-
stricting and distasteful, he soon resigned his place.

In 1836, after he had settled in the village of Concord, he published his first book, a thin volume entitled
Nature, which was the product of years of meditation and
which contains the ground plan of his philosophy. Shortly
afterwards he joined a group of his neighbors and friends
in an organization later to be known as the Transcendental
Club. The first meeting was held in Boston, at the home of
George Ripley, and the second in Concord, at Emerson's

37

house. Besides these two, the more prominent members included Bronson Alcott, Frederic Henry Hedge, Orestes Brownson, James Freeman Clarke, Theodore Parker, and Margaret Fuller. They met at irregular intervals for seven or eight years, and sponsored the publication of *The Dial* for the brief duration of its lifetime, 1840 to 1844.

The origins of the transcendental movement are not easy to define. The immediate precipitant, probably, was the philosophy of the German idealists, Kant, Fichte, and Schelling, as it was reported and augmented in the writings of Coleridge and Carlyle. These young men, several of whom were ministers, were eager for new ideas wherever they might be found, and it is certain that they were found in the writings of Plato, Plotinus, and the English Platonists, as well as among the more advanced thinkers of their own time. Whatever borrowings there may have been, however, transcendentalism was to a large extent the product, as I have said already, of the evolution of Puritanism. It may be helpful at this point, therefore, to review briefly the development of the concepts of God and man from Calvinism to Emerson.

Calvinism places God and man at opposite poles. God is infinitely high and man is infinitely low; God is the arbitrary sovereign, man the groveling subject. But man is not utterly shut off from God, for God bestows grace upon a few individuals whom he chooses to lift out of depravity and draw to himself. The means by which this grace is made possible is Christ's death and resurrection. By reason of God's mystic three-fold unity, he is able to remain God and at the same time become man in Christ, thus uniting the two extremes of man and God in the second person of the Trinity. But of course Calvinism permitted this union

with God to only a few, and even for them it is not a perfect union, because a distinction is made between the
Christ-man and the ordinary man. Christ becomes man
temporarily to achieve God's purpose, and then with-
draws again into heaven.

The first step away from this absolutism was taken by
Arminianism, which affirmed that Christ atoned for all,
and that therefore all men might, through belief in Christ,
attain that union with God which Calvinism had denied to
all except the elect. The doctrine of salvation through
man's faith rather than through God's grace allowed man
the freedom of will which Edwards had denied him. This
step from determinism to free will in Protestant doctrine
was bitterly contested for two hundred years. Deism,
though not in the direct line of change, was a parallel development and doubtless instrumental in preparing the
way for Unitarianism, which was the next step. Unitarianism denied the doctrine of the Trinity and, in its more
liberal form, defined Christ as a man, albeit a great and
wise man, meant to be the teacher and leader of other
men. The last step was transcendentalism, which brings
us to the fully matured Emerson and is best exemplified
in his own thought.

Since American idealism in its modern phase was formulated by Emerson and yet survives, outside the schools
at any rate, as Emersonian idealism, it is necessary to
examine the main features of his philosophy. We may begin with his concepts of God, of nature, and of man. He
conceived God as the universal soul, not a force or a person outside the universe. Like the Unitarians he believed
this soul to be one and not three. Christ was the soul indi-
vidualized, and was therefore a man essentially like other

men. Christ saw the mystery of the soul and lived and had his being in the soul; he was God incarnated in the individual. And Emerson believed that what Christ was, every man may become. In short, Emerson believed that every man is an incarnation of God, although of course men express God incompletely and in different degrees. For God is the soul, and there are not two orders of souls, human and divine, but one universal soul which reveals itself in many individual forms. Man is not altogether soul, however; he has a body and is therefore a part of nature. Hence to understand Emerson's concept of man we must examine his concept of nature.

"Philosophically considered," he says in the introduction to *Nature*, "the universe is composed of Nature and the Soul." This is the same as to say that the universe is composed of matter and mind, a statement to which all philosophers can agree. What philosophers disagree upon is the relation between matter and mind. Some have believed that they are mutually independent and coexistent realities; these were dualists in the strict sense of the word. They contended that if matter ceased to exist mind would continue as before, unchanged, and that if mind ceased to exist the material world would likewise continue unchanged. Opposed to the dualists were the monists, who believed that mind and matter do not exist as we know them separately in a dual world but are essentially one. But there were two kinds of monists. One school affirmed matter to be the only reality and explained mind as a development or phenomenon of matter; these were the materialists. The other school affirmed mind to be the only reality, and explained matter as a manifestation or phenomenon of mind; these were the idealists.

Emerson was strongly attracted by the last of these philosophies, the idealistic. "Idealism," he writes, "sees the world in God. It beholds the whole circle of persons and things, of actions and events, of country and religion, not as painfully accumulated, atom after atom, act after act, in an aged creeping Past, but as one vast picture which God paints on the instant eternity for the contemplation of the soul." In another place he calls nature "the apparition of God." Emerson is unwilling to accept as final, however, a theory that denies the existence of matter. "It leaves me," he complained, "in the splendid labyrinth of my perceptions, to wander without end." It makes nature foreign to man and does not account for the fact that man is conscious of some relation between himself and nature. He is willing to accept the theory of idealism only as a "useful introductory hypothesis" which serves "to apprize us of the eternal distinction between the soul and the world." The hypothesis answers the question, What is matter? but it does not explain the whole meaning of nature.

There remain to be answered still the questions Whence is matter? and Whereto? Emerson says the answers to these questions rise out of the recesses of consciousness and are known by intuition. Nature, he discovers, is the creation of spirit, but spirit is a power within nature, not outside of it, and also within the soul of man. This spirit, which is the Supreme Being, "does not build up nature around us, but puts it forth through us, as the life of the tree puts forth new branches and leaves through the pores of the old. As a plant upon the earth, so a man rests upon the bosom of God; he is nourished by unfailing fountains, and draws at his need inexhaustible power."

Nature, it therefore appears, is, like man, an incarnation of God; but man is an incarnation in the realm of consciousness, whereas nature is an incarnation in the realm of the unconscious. Since nature is not subject to the human will it has not degenerated but stands as originally created, a perfect exposition and illustration of the divine mind. The laws of nature are the laws of God under the limitation of matter, and in so far as man exists within the sphere of these laws, he must obey them. This is the meaning he gives to Fate. Fate is nature, circumstance, what a man may do now; it "is a name for facts not yet passed under the fire of thought; for causes which are unpenetrated."

Thus he explains the origin and present condition of nature. But whereto? What is it for? How does he answer his third question? He answers it by saying that nature is a discipline for the understanding in intellectual truths. Science seeks to understand nature and in the process improves the intellect of the scientist. Nature is also a discipline for the reason in moral truths. The reason reveals behind the physical laws of nature the universal moral law which gives it unity. This distinction between the understanding and the reason derives from Kant and was popularized by Coleridge. By means of the understanding the human mind wins a gradual and painful mastery of the laws of nature for material ends; by means of the reason it becomes one with that spirit which is the living source of all laws and masters them to spiritual ends. It is the power of the reason that reveals nature as the picture which God "paints on the instant eternity for the contemplation of the soul."

It is quite evident that Emerson will not accept without qualification the theory that matter does not exist, even though he calls nature an apparition of God. Was he then a dualist, a believer in the separate existence of two independent substances? I find no evidence of the fact. So far as I know the word "dual" occurs nowhere in his writings except in the essay "Fate," in which he states that Fate and Power are the opposite sides of a dual world; but this is only the distinction made in the introduction to *Nature*, previously referred to, between the soul (which is Power) and nature (which is Fate). The word "dualism" occurs twice. We find it first in the chapter on "Idealism" in *Nature*, where he applies the term to "the difference between the observer and the spectacle —between man and nature"; a difference whereby man becomes aware of the fact "that whilst the world is a spectacle, something in himself is stable." This is the experience in which the mind is made aware both of itself and of its object, but recognizes the mind as the only reality. The other instance of the use of the term occurs in the essay "Compensation," where he uses it as a synonym of "polarity." Since the word "polarity" appears frequently in Emerson's writings and may be an important clue to his meaning, it is necessary to examine his use of it with care.

The word is borrowed from the science of physics, where it is common enough; but Emerson extends its use to metaphysics and even to ethics. It appears first, I believe, in "The American Scholar" in the following passage:

> *That great principle of Undulation in nature, that shows itself in the inspiring and expiring of the breath;*

in desire and satiety; in the ebb and flow of the sea; in day and night; in heat and cold; and, as yet more deeply ingrained in every atom and every fluid, is known to us under the name of Polarity,—these "fits of easy transmission and reflection," as Newton called them, are the law of nature because they are the law of spirit.

In nature, also, appear such opposites as action and reaction, male and female, and the centrifugal and centripetal forces of heavenly bodies. These polarities are to be found in each part and particle of nature.

In making polarity a law of nature because it is a law of spirit, Emerson extends it beyond nature into the realm of being, and so gives to it a metaphysical character. We may expand his statement to mean that spirit is the universal cause, which can be known only by the reason, and nature the particular effect, which can be known by the understanding. This interpretation is confirmed by the following application of the law of polarity in "Compensation":

Every act rewards itself, or in other words integrates itself, in a twofold manner; first in the thing, or in real nature; and secondly in the circumstance, or in apparent nature. Men call the circumstance the retribution. The casual retribution is in the thing, and is seen by the soul. The retribution in the circumstance is seen by the understanding; it is inseparable from the thing, but is often spread over a long time and so does not become distinct until after many years. . . . Cause and effect, means and ends, seed and fruit, cannot be severed; for the effect already blooms in the cause, the end preëxists in the means, the fruit in the seed.

What he refers to here as "real nature" is the same as what elsewhere he calls soul, spirit, or mind; and what he refers to as "apparent nature" is the same thing that he sometimes calls simply nature, or matter. In the essay on "Fate" he explains history as the action and reaction of nature and thought. This perpetual conflict between mind and matter has produced the universal belief in a good spirit and a wicked spirit who are eternally at war. Emerson does not deny the reality of this conflict, but he sees the conflicting powers as the complementary aspects of a cosmic unity. Formerly it was believed that spirit is divine and matter diabolic, but science and philosophy have taught us to see "how each reflects the other as face answers to face in a glass: nay, how the laws of both are one, or how one is the realization."

This opposition or polarity of mind and matter in cosmic unity is repeated in lesser units throughout the realm of organic life. The higher the organism in the scale of life, the less rigid is the rule of law; in the highest organism, man, matter becomes plastic and is shaped by mind into a likeness of itself. Thus the individual man is a microcosm in which mind and matter, the soul and nature, constitute an organic unity which is, on the level of individuality, identical with the unity of the cosmos. Within the microcosmic individual the law of polarity prevails as elsewhere. This relation of the individual to the universe is described by Emerson in the following words:

An individual body is the momentary arrest or fixation of certain atoms, which, after performing compulsory duty to this enchanted statue, are released again to flow in the currents of the world. An individual mind in like

manner is a fixation or momentary eddy in which certain
services and powers are taken up and minister in petty
niches and localities, and then, being released, return to
the unbounded soul of the world.

The body of man, because it is a fixation of certain
atoms, is subject to the law of nature; whereas the mind
of man, because it is a fixation of certain powers drawn
from the soul of the world, is subject to the law of spirit.
An individual man is the fruit of the ages, but he has not
yet become the assured master of his environment. The
law that established nature and the human race contin-
ually thwarts the will of ignorant individuals; for a man
is but a fixation of brute atoms until he thinks, and then
he uses them as he will. It is not that he escapes the law of
nature, but that in the light of knowledge he discovers
the law of nature to be one with the law of spirit. Man is
an infinite soul, and both heaven and earth are passing
into his mind; he is aware of an intellect that overhangs
his consciousness like a sky, and if he receives this intellect
into himself, he is able to do with knowledge what the
stones do by structure under natural law. Intellect is
power; it frees man from the limitation of fate. But he
must always maintain the mind in a state of freedom or
else the iron laws of fate will close upon him again.

The moral sentiment also frees man from the law of
nature, or rather it places him in a state of harmony with
it. The moral sentiment makes man aware that the perfect
law of duty is reflected in the laws of chemistry, vegeta-
tion, and astronomy. The law which is only a negation
and a limitation in nature is made alive in the human
mind; it is inspiration. The moral sentiment, in short,

centers, concentrates us; it "puts us at the heart of Nature, where we belong, in the cabinet of science and of causes, there where all the wires terminate which hold the world in magnetic unity, and so converts us into universal beings." Thus it is that through the intellect and the moral sentiment the individual rises from the lower levels of life, where he was shut in and constrained by the laws of nature, which are Fate, into the higher level of life, where he breathes the freedom of God-like unity and universality. Under the law of polarity, says Emerson, man is

a stupendous antagonism, a dragging together of the poles of the Universe. . . . On one side elemental order, sandstone and granite, rock-ledges, peat-bog, forest, sea and shore; and on the other part thought, the spirit which composes and decomposes nature,—here they are, side by side, god and devil, mind and matter, king and conspirator, belt and spasm, riding peacefully together in the eye and brain of every man.

In the common possession of this universal spirit all men are made equal. Emerson thinks that the philosophy of the past, which has stressed the distinction between individuals and not the universal attributes of man, is an impoverishing philosophy. The moral sentiment, he says, equalizes all because it bestows spiritual wealth and power. This doctrine of the identity of the individual with the universal in spiritual power means that "what is best in each kind is an index of what should be the average of that thing." It was his faith that the moral sentiment would instruct each person in the law of his own nature, which is the universal law, and which has throughout na-

ture a uniform purpose, namely, "to make the best better and the worst good." This purpose could not be possible except on the assumption of spiritual equality deriving
from the presence of the universal in the individual.

It is through the individual, of course, that the law of
polarity makes itself effective in ethics, the sphere of human relationships. The two poles of matter and spirit,
which can be united and harmonized in the individual,
draw apart again when one individual has to deal with
another or a group. Here there is not that unconscious
drawing together of separate elements by a common law
as in objective nature. As the whole has its law, so each
individual has his special genius, which sets him apart
from other individuals. This determination of genius is
so strong that it would make society impossible if it were
not held in check by other forces which draw men together for their common advantage. As it is, men are best
and most by themselves, and when they are compelled to
work together they work with diminished power. Nature
provides for the protection of the individual's sacred identity against the will of other individuals to expand and
draw him into the circle of their power. But the individual
of limited power cannot escape the influence of great men,
and should not wish to. The spirit of a great man diffuses
itself beyond the limits of his personality. He seems, to
his admirers, at first a complete and original spirit, a
cause; but presently, as they grow in understanding, he
will be seen in a truer light as the exponent of a mind and
will vaster than his own. He will be seen as an effect, not
a cause, and then his admirers can look through him to
the First Cause from which he has drawn his power. And
not only that. In seeing him against the background of

the universal spirit, they see themselves in him, and they see that all which he now is they may become if only they can realize their powers. The hero whom the youth admires is only a projection of his own soul.

This conception of the individual and of the hero involves a kind of aristocracy of character which at first appears to contradict Emerson's democratic principles, but the contradiction is more apparent than real. He believes that aristocracy is inevitable; for if the majority should destroy the more gifted minority, a new group of superior persons will rise from among those who remain, as surely as cream rises in a bowl of milk; and though class after class be destroyed until only two men are left, one would be the leader and would be involuntarily obeyed and imitated by the other. His view is that an aristocracy is justified so long as it depends upon merit. Men of superior qualities become eminent and constitute a standard for emulation. "Men of aim must lead the aimless," he declares; "men of invention the uninventive." Those who become leaders must be catholic men who "carry the world in their thoughts." At the conclusion of his essay on "Aristocracy" he describes the type of American man who might be justly called a gentleman or man of honor in a democratic society:

Call it man of honor, or call it Man, the American who would serve his country must learn the beauty and honor of perseverance, he must reinforce himself by the power of character, and revisit the margin of that well from which his fathers drew waters of life and enthusiasm, the fountain I mean of the moral sentiments, the parent fountain from which this goodly Universe flows as a wave.

For Emerson, then, character, which is grounded in the moral sentiment, rather than intellect qualifies an individual in a democratic society for leadership. The man of character will never use his power for selfish ends, but always for the good of the people and for the purpose of assisting them to reach his own moral elevation.

The moral sentiment, functioning as character in individual persons, is the foundation of society. All governments, and democratic governments in particular, have their origin in the moral identity of men. The virtues of a community or a state are never greater, and in fact are always less, than the virtues of the citizens who constitute it. "Is not a man better than a town?" Emerson demands. He is, of course, because in associating himself with others he subjects himself to the limits of some kind of organization. "Every spirit makes its house," he says; "but afterwards the house confines the spirit." It is one of the contradictions of our world that men as a group can advance only by means of institutions, and yet every such institution finally becomes an obstacle to further advance. This is the reason Emerson, like many other individualists of his generation, desired as little government as possible. "The appearance of character makes the State unnecessary," he insisted. "The wise man is the State." The individual who resists the state's encroachment upon his liberty is an antidote to the abuse of government. The state is the opposite of the individual as nature is the opposite of the soul; they are perpetual antagonists perpetually reconciled and inseparable. They are the two poles of the human community. But the creative power resides in the individual, not in the state, and the individual is, as Emerson has said, best and most when alone. It is only the individual who dreams and hopes for better things, and what his imagination builds on airy foundations will eventually be enacted by legislative assemblies. Hence we may be certain that every man is better than the system he creates. Always the new life is concealed in the bud. "Behind every individual closes organization; before him opens liberty,—the Better, the Best."

This propensity of the individual to be forever creating new forms and abandoning the old has been characteristic especially of the frontier, whether physical or mental, in all times and places of human development. The great moment in history, Emerson pointed out, is when the savage is just ceasing to be a savage. "Everything good in nature and the world is in that moment of transition, when the swarthy juices still flow plentifully from nature, but their astringency or acridity is got out by ethics and humanity." Such a moment was the age of Pericles in ancient Greece, and, in some measure, such was the first half of the nineteenth century in the United States. Emerson limits the period from 1820 to 1840. "There are always two parties," he said, "the party of the Past and the party of the Future; the Establishment and the Movement." America was of the party of the future, the party of movement. He was not altogether happy with America as he found it, calling it superficial, a nation of shopkeepers. But he was not discouraged. "The way to mend the bad world," he remarked, "is to create the right world." He pointed out the fact that in his day America was at the beginning, not the meridian, of its development, and he looked to the future with great expectations. "Here is man," he said, "in the Garden of Eden; here the Genesis and the Exodus." It was indeed like setting up a new order of life that might hope to equal in sublimity the geographical setting in which it was placed. Emerson was fully aware of the continued materialism of the American people and their lack of what he termed "male energy," by which he meant intellectual and moral power. Yet he realized that "material and moral values are always commensurate" and that "every material organization exists to a moral end, which makes the reason of its existence."

He admitted that he had little esteem for governments, putting the private man first always, and arguing that he who is not able to stand alone is not qualified to be a citizen. The reason for the state's existence is to execute the will of its citizens, and it should be changed whenever it fails thus to justify its existence. Many are in fact citizens, he realized, who cannot stand alone, but he knew that they would acquire the power to stand alone only if permitted to make the attempt and helped in their struggle for self-improvement. He was not among those who would limit government merely to a police power. "The tendencies of the times," he wrote, "favor the idea of self-government. . . . It promises a recognition of higher rights than those of personal freedom, or the security of property. A man has a right to be employed, to be trusted, to be loved, to be revered." Those citizens who enjoy peculiar and legitimate advantages should take delight in securing these advantages for all, otherwise they are not true patriots. The end of political government, he believed, is not democracy; that is only the means. Morality is the true end, a state of things which allows every man the largest liberty compatible with the liberty of every other man. He would have government more tender and paternal: "more thoughtful for the interests of

women, for the training of children, and for the welfare of sick and unable persons, and serious care of crim-
inals, than was ever any the best government of the Old
World." Nor must America be content to live to herself
and care only for her own. He wished to see America "a
benefactor such as no country ever was, hospitable to all
nations, legislating for all nationalities." There is surely
no comfort in these words for isolationists and laissez-
faire economists.

Before concluding this chapter, it may be well to recall what has been said earlier in this essay about Jonathan
Edwards and Benjamin Franklin. Edwards was described
as an idealist who hoped for the perfection of the individual by spiritual improvement. Franklin was described
as a pragmatist who hoped for the perfection of society by
material improvement. This categorical distinction is un-
fair to both men because it makes them appear more narrow than they were, but it serves to illustrate the two
sides of the typical American character. The ideal and the
practical are polar opposites, like mind and matter, but
both are present and necessary in the temperament of
every individual, though usually one predominates. Emerson had more of the idealism of Edwards than of the
practicality of Franklin, but he was by no means imprac-
tical; and the purpose of his life was to popularize a philosophy which might make these two qualities combine
harmoniously in the individual and in society.

As Emerson conceived it, idealism included and provided for pragmatism somewhat in the same manner as
his concept of the soul included and provided for nature.
Speaking to the Phi Beta Kappa Society at Cambridge in
1867, he said:

We wish to put the ideal rules into practice, to offer liberty instead of chains, and see whether liberty will not disclose its proper checks; believing that a free press will prove safer than the censorship; to ordain free trade, and believe that it will not bankrupt us; universal suffrage, believing that it will not carry us to mobs, or back to kings again. I believe the checks are as sure as the springs.

Ideals, therefore, can be put to practical use, in Emerson's opinion, but they cannot be made to go beyond the people who use them. The state, as well as the individual, rests on an ideal basis, but it is the individual who builds the state. "We surround ourselves always, according to our freedom and ability," he said, "with true images of ourselves in things." The state is a composite image of all its citizens, and if the reformer would improve the state he must begin with the individuals who compose it. Since, in Emerson's faith, there is no limit to man's power to improve himself, there is likewise no limit to his power to improve the world in which he lives.

IV

Contemporaries of Emerson

Through the development of idealism in American thought from its seventeenth-century beginnings to its culmination in the philosophy of Emerson, man was lifted out of the depravity to which Calvinistic theology condemned him into a position of dignity and power, and clothed with divinity. From being an object of God's wrath he came to feel himself an instrument of God's power. He who had supposed himself an outcast now discovered that he was sovereign of the world. This change in the concept of the individual man implied a change in the concept of man in communities. To a people believing in the fatalistic doctrines of Calvin a democratic society was impossible, whereas to a people imbued with the faith of Emerson it seemed inevitable.

Emerson was aware that the forces which were slowly building a democratic society in America had made great progress in the two centuries preceding him, and he was also aware that he was himself, in part, a product of those forces. Yet he was not content with what had been accomplished, desiring to push on more rapidly towards his ideal. One might almost believe that he sensed the coming lapse of moral power in America and the consequent interruption of democratic evolution, and that he was building up the power of the individual, knowing that when institutions fail, then more than ever should the individual stand firm.

There was no lack of new ideas and new movements in his generation. It was an age of projects. Probably more religious sects, political creeds, and pseudo-sciences came into existence and gained a popular following during the second quarter of the nineteenth century in the United States than ever happened in a comparable period of time before or since anywhere on the face of the globe. Transcendentalism was in some respects a part of this restless groping for something new and marvelous, and among its adherents there were a few cranks as well as some wise men and clever women. Of the cranks, there is no need to take further notice. Of the wise men and clever women there were such interesting examples as Bronson Alcott, whose conversation was profound and enchanting but could never be reduced to clear and unadulterated sense; Theodore Parker, the energetic evangel of transcendentalism who was master of twenty languages and who said, "I wish to stand on the earth, though I would look beyond the stars"; and Margaret Fuller, feminist, editor, and critic, whose hunger for ideas was insatiable, whose talk was brilliant and endless, and whose rebellious temperament kept her in hot water constantly. These and perhaps a dozen others, members of the Transcendental Club, made such an intellectual stir as had never been dreamed of before in the environs of Boston. But the best of their thinking as transcendentalists is summarized in the writings of Emerson, and the rest is of little consequence to the history of idealism.

There were others among Emerson's contemporaries who were, like him, idealists and heirs of Puritanism, but who differed from him in one important way or another. We must not assume that all people of that time were transcendentalists; in fact only a handful were, and they were not the most influential leaders among the common people and in the everyday affairs of life. In order that we may follow the course of idealism in American literature and see it in all its phases, we must now consider briefly the other important literary men in the first half of the past century.

John Greenleaf Whittier was a Massachusetts farmer, a natural democrat and a Quaker, in whom the heritage of many generations of piety and sturdy individualism found poetic expression. He was by temperament gentle, benevolent, and sentimental rather than passionate and intellectual, and it was only his outraged sense of human dignity that roused him to a passionate opposition to slavery. He could never have analyzed the problem of slavery from its economic effects; it was a degradation of human nature, and that was sufficient to condemn it forever and completely in his eyes. His chief value for us is in his idyllic pictures of New England country life before the rise of industrialism. In showing us the dignity and lovableness of plain people he strengthened our faith in democracy.

Another New Englander who was skeptical of Emerson's philosophy and impatient with everything that smacked of mysticism was Oliver Wendell Holmes, physician, humorist, and inveterate enemy of Calvinism. He may be called an ethical idealist, but he was a child of the eighteenth century and more at home among the rationalists and neo-classicists than among the transcendentalists and romanticists. He knew nothing of the Jacksonian frontier democracy that was growing up in the West, and liked to boast that "Boston State-House is the hub of the solar system." In his belief that "science represents the thought of God discovered by man" he reminds us somewhat of Emerson. Like Emerson, he often drew images from nature to illustrate his opinions. One of the most famous instances of this use of nature is the well known poem "The Chambered Nautilus," which expresses the idea that the soul creates the forms by which it lives; it is therefore closer to the idealism of Emerson than probably Holmes himself would have liked to admit. It is only fair to say, however, that this poem is not characteristic of Holmes. It is by his humor rather than by his more serious work that Holmes is remembered, and perhaps we are fortunate that this is so, for humor was a rare commodity in New England literature before his time. A democratic society must have a robust humor to balance the serious side of its idealism. Holmes' skepticism, because it is good-humored, is stimulating rather than destructive.

Henry Wadsworth Longfellow, like Holmes, was inclined towards an aristocratic view of life. Emerson complained in his *Journal*: "If Socrates were here, we could go and talk with him; but Longfellow, we cannot go and talk with; there is a palace, and servants, and a row of bottles of different coloured wines, and wine glasses, and fine coats." Nevertheless, as we all know, Longfellow has been and still is the most popular of the older poets in our literature. The reason for this popularity is not hard to discover. His was an idealism of romance and sentiment rather than of intellectual and moral force, and he never troubles us with new ideas or realistic situations. He asks us to look with him through a twilight haze of sentiment and fancy into the past, which is always the past of tradition and nostalgic memory, and in the mildly melancholy mood of reminiscence we are drawn away from the unpleasant realities of today and the unsolved problems of tomorrow. He strokes us the right way when we are worried and we grow complacent. He has also identified himself in such poems as "A Psalm of Life" with the noble, if somewhat vague, aspirations of adolescent Americans, and has helped to sustain their faith through trial and disappointment. There is a genuine usefulness in such poems, and those who carp at them because under closer examination they prove to be vague and trite fail to understand that a simple person who is emotionally unsettled may find haze and platitudes more comforting than disturbing ideas.

Longfellow has also been of service in translating and idealizing certain passages in the history of our country. The youth who has absorbed *Evangeline*, *Hiawatha*, and *The Courtship of Miles Standish* at the proper stage of his cultural development is a better citizen for the experience, albeit he may discover afterwards that these famous poems are not quite the masterpieces of literature that he had taken them to be. Emerson's formula for democracy requires the cultivation of the affections of the heart, and nothing is more adapted to this function than the poetry of Longfellow. It may be said, therefore, that although Longfellow contributed nothing original to the theory of democracy, he has had a share in developing the sentiments and the affections appropriate to a democratic people.

The three writers just discussed were only a few years

younger than Emerson and could not have been expected to be influenced by him. James Russell Lowell, however, was sixteen years younger than Emerson, and when he was a boy of nineteen he was sent from college to spend several weeks in Concord, where he met Emerson and walked with him. It pleased his youthful egotism to think lightly of Emerson at that time, although he had already heard the famous "American Scholar" address and been impressed by it, but when he was older he did not neglect to praise him. Lowell was like Longfellow, only more robust, more practical, and less sentimental. He had Longfellow's love of the past, of learning, of moral teaching, but he was more humorous than Longfellow, more interested in public affairs, and more appreciative of the virtues of the common man. He has been criticized for lack of firmness and independence in his opinions. In his early youth he was inclined to be conservative like his father; then he met and married Maria White, whose zeal for abolitionism infected him with the germ of radicalism which continued largely to govern his thoughts and actions until after her death in 1853; afterwards he became in some ways more conservative, although he never reverted to the Federalist views of his youth.

By birth and breeding he belonged to the aristocracy of Boston, but he has given us some of the most powerful interpretations of the sturdy, homespun character of the New England countryman that are to be found in our literature. The most notable of his productions in this style are the two series of the *Biglow Papers*, written in New England dialect. In his "Harvard Commemoration Ode" he has incorporated a tribute to Lincoln that does credit to the subject. Of the work of his later years, the address on "Democracy," which he delivered at Birmingham, England, in 1884, is justly admired, although some of his American critics thought he catered to English opinion. "Our healing," he said, "is not in the storm or in the whirlwind, it is not in monarchies, or aristocracies, or democracies, but will be revealed by the still, small voice that speaks to the conscience and the heart, prompting us to a wider and wiser humanity." The reference to the voice of conscience shows that Lowell was a Puritan and a spiritual kinsman of Emerson, and yet this passage also suggests that he has been rightly classified not as an idealist or a realist, a democrat or an aristocrat, but rather as a humanist. He had Emerson's love of humanity, but not his steady faith in the ultimate wisdom of the individual man.

While Emerson in New England was formulating a theory of truth during the years between 1830 and 1840, Edgar Allan Poe in Virginia was formulating a theory of beauty that is closely parallel to it. Poe sometimes scoffed at the theories of transcendentalists and supposed his own idea to be antithetical to theirs. Nevertheless they had much in common. If beauty be substituted for truth, Poe's search for the transcendent is much like that of Emerson. Poe saw in the beauty of nature a means by which the mind is led to a conception of absolute beauty, and he believed that in the realm of the absolute, beauty and truth are one. In his early poem "Al Aaraaf," Poe symbolizes truth in the pure ray of white light and beauty in the colors of the spectrum. The white light, truth, and the colored light, beauty, are merely two aspects of the same ray. It may be said, therefore, that although Emerson and Poe travelled by different paths, they meant to arrive at the same destination, one by the way of truth and the other by the way of beauty.

Where in Emerson we find the moral sentiment, in Poe we find the sentiment of poesy, which he defines as the soul's desire for supernal beauty. Poe identified this poetic sentiment, or love of the beautiful, with the human instinct of veneration. The soul is not content merely to perceive and appreciate beauty; it longs to possess and become one with it. There is, Poe believed, an excitement or elevation of the soul in the contemplation of beauty that is parallel to the exaltation of the soul of the religious mystic in the contemplation of goodness or truth. This excitement of the soul stimulates the faculty of intuition, which he identifies with the imagination. "Imagination is, possibly in man," says Poe, "a lesser degree of the creative power in God." He thinks the imagination brings the soul of the individual into a very close relationship with the universal, so that it has glimpses of "things supernal and eternal." He says, further, "Some of the most profound knowledge—perhaps all *very* profound knowledge—has originated from a highly stimulated imagination." If we read "intuition" instead of "imagination" we have the transcendental theory in its essence.

A year or two before his death Poe wrote an essay—he called it a prose-poem—entitled *Eureka*, in which he proposed an explanation of the universe. I shall not attempt here an exposition of this remarkable essay except to point out its central idea; namely, that mind is consistency, and consistency is truth; that the universe is symmetry, and symmetry is beauty; that symmetry and consistency are convertible terms; and that therefore beauty and truth are one. It would be more accurate, perhaps, to say that beauty and truth are two attributes of one identical essence. "We may take for granted then," he says, "that man cannot long or widely err, if he suffer himself to be guided by his poetical, which I have maintained to be his truthful, in being his symmetrical, instinct."

Manifestly it would be a mistake to exclude Poe from the company of American writers who have fostered the theory of idealism in America. He was willing to acknowledge that God is truth; but he insisted that God is beauty also, and that through his attribute of beauty he evokes the instinct or sentiment of beauty in the individual soul, and so unites the individual with himself. Whatever may have been their differences in point of view and manner of speech, both Emerson and Poe believed that the soul of man is able to rise above the limitations of nature, through truth according to the one and through beauty according to the other, and achieve union with the universal. Both felt that the human understanding inevitably misled man into half-truths; Emerson turned to the "reason" for guidance, Poe to the "imagination." But by "reason" Emerson intended the intuitive sense, and by "imagination" Poe intended the same. It is odd that they should have been so totally incapable of understanding each other, since both were searching for perfection through ways transcendental.

We turn now to the work of two great American writers who could not so readily free themselves from the fatal limitations of nature, and whose explorations were through the subterranean shadows of the soul rather than in its sunlit ways. These two writers were Nathaniel Hawthorne, who was but one year younger than Emerson, and Herman Melville, who was two years younger than Thoreau. Although they were not, strictly speaking, transcendentalists, they were products of the same Puritan culture that produced Emerson and Thoreau, and they were, like them, persevering students of the mysteries of the soul. Like Emerson they identified fate with the laws of nature, but unlike him they found no sure ground for believing that the soul can transcend the limitation of fate.

Hawthorne's conception of the limitation which the laws of matter impose upon the powers of the mind is powerfully illustrated in many of his stories, but most directly perhaps in "The Birthmark." This is a short story of a brilliant scientist, Aylmer, who marries a woman whose beauty he thinks would be perfect if it were not for a small birthmark, hardly noticeable to others, in the middle of one cheek. It becomes for him "the visible mark of earthly imperfection," and he is so obsessed with the thought that both husband and wife are made very unhappy. Finally she agrees to permit him to try to remove the mark. He succeeds, but in the moment it disappears and the physical beauty of the woman is made perfect, she dies. At that moment the scientist's servant, a faithful but ugly and animal-like man, gives vent to a hoarse, chuckling laugh of triumph. The scientist is obviously the type of mind or spirit, and his servant is the type of matter, which, though the servant of mind, is its opposite and its limitation. Clearly the story is a warning to the idealist that it is fatal to ground his faith in material perfection. "Thus ever," comments the author, "does the gross fatality of earth exult in its invariable triumph over the immortal essence which, in this sphere of half development, demands the completeness of a higher state." Hawthorne does not relegate the spirit to utter hopelessness, however, for he concludes his story with the following comment:

Yet, had Aylmer reached a profounder wisdom, he need not thus have flung away the happiness which would have woven his mortal life of the selfsame texture with the celestial. The momentary circumstance was too strong for him; he failed to look beyond the shadowy scope of time, and, living once for all in eternity, to find the perfect future in the present.

In other words, if the scientist had lived in the eternity of spirit and grounded his happiness there instead of in material perfection, he would have found that the hoped-for perfection of the future becomes the possession of the present. This is very close to Emerson's teaching that the virtuous soul draws nature into itself and is thereby freed from its limitation.

It will be remembered that Emerson many times stated that the realm of nature is one of law because the realm of spirit is one of law. It is as if spirit should impress its structure upon matter. This is the law of polarity, or as he sometimes called it, compensation. There is no escape from it for the individual; but if the individual takes the law into himself and identifies himself with the universal spirit, he becomes a free soul and feels no conflict.

Hawthorne's great novel, *The Scarlet Letter*, illustrates this Emersonian doctrine perfectly. Hester Prynne, who was already a wife, and Arthur Dimmesdale, a minister, violate the moral law and the law of the community in the sin of adultery. Hester cannot escape the penalty of her sin, because she bears a child, and the child is nature's witness to her guilt. The community imposes its penalty upon her, and she is made to stand in public disgrace on the town scaffold and wear a scarlet letter A on her bosom. Moreover, the child is a perpetual reminder and quickener of conscience. But the minister does not stand upon the scaffold, and his guilt is not known. It looks as if he will escape the penalty of sin. But not so. In the end he not only stands in public disgrace on the scaffold, driven there by his conscience, but he dies there; and the stigma of his guilt, the scarlet letter A, is branded upon his flesh over the heart, or so it is said by some of the witnesses. In reality, Hawthorne's purpose does not call for the stigma upon Dimmesdale's flesh, and the author implies that those who thought they saw it there only imagined it was there. The letter, as he says, is branded upon his inmost heart, his soul. Hester's executioners, like the child that was the evidence of her guilt, were extrinsic facts existing in the realm of nature, whereas Dimmesdale's executioner and the evidence of his guilt were both intrinsic facts hidden to all except himself; they were within his own soul, but they were none the less fatal for that. It was only by paying the price exacted both in nature and in the realm of spirit that his soul won peace. That price was the sacrifice of earthly life and happiness. Not only must the soul abide by the laws of nature in so far as it lives in nature, but it must also obey its own laws. This is the meaning of Dimmesdale's tragedy.

Another idea that Hawthorne had in common with Emerson is that the intellect becomes the very essence of evil when divorced from the affections, which spring from the moral sentiment. This is illustrated in *The Scarlet Letter* in the person of Roger Chillingworth, who in the fiendish pursuit of his revenge upon Dimmesdale actually becomes a fiend. The idea is here complicated, however, by the fact that Chillingworth hates Dimmesdale. In one of the short stories, "Rappaccini's Daughter," the element of hate is absent. Dr. Rappaccini experimented with his daughter by feeding her from infancy upon poisonous flowers, so graduated that eventually she became immune to the poisons. What is more remarkable, her body at last came to be as poisonous as the flowers themselves and even to require the poisons for its continued existence. The object of the experiment was to make a discovery that would benefit mankind, but it failed, and the girl's life was sacrificed. The moral is that the power of the intellect is a power of evil unless it be tempered by the human affections. In general, the lesson that Hawthorne would have us learn is that being the creatures of love, we should obey love's injunctions, and being the children of nature, we must abide by the laws of nature. We can have the freedom of the soul only in the exclusive realm of the spirit.

Melville, like Hawthorne, explored the dark side of the soul rather than the bright side; he too stressed the soul's limitations more than its freedom, or perhaps I should say he emphasized the futility of attempting to express the soul in terms of mind. Again like Hawthorne, he felt an instinctive antagonism to the transcendental philosophy, although he was more than half a transcendentalist himself. He was unlike Hawthorne, however, and unlike all the others of his generation in his violent rebellion against the limitations of fate. The problem of the individual, of God, and of being itself would not let him rest, although he could never find any solution for it. The idea of being annihilates the idea of the individual, and the idea of the individual is a doorless cell from which there is no escape into the wider freedom of being. Writing to Hawthorne in March, 1851, he said: "But it is this *Being* of the matter; there lies the knot with which we choke ourselves. As soon as you say *Me*, a *God*, a *Nature*, so soon you jump off from your stool and hang from the beam. Yes, that word is the hangman. Take God out of the dictionary, and you would have Him in the street."

Melville is saying that when you build a wall around a part of being, as you must do when you attempt to define it as *Me*, a separate self, or a *God* or a *Nature*, which are also separate and individual entities, you necessarily destroy the universality and immortality of being. Man's loss of universality is related in the familiar story of Adam in the book of Genesis. Adam before he ate the forbidden fruit was generic man, not *a* man, not a separate soul; he was therefore one with God, universal and immortal. The generic man includes woman also, but even when woman, Eve, was taken from Adam, man, as one side of his dual nature, the two together were still generic man, and there was yet no separation from God. Separation was the consequence of man's becoming an individual soul and exercising an individual will, or perhaps it would be better to say that the individual soul was born or created in the moment of separation. The separation and loss of unity was the death which was meant when God told Adam and Eve that if they ate the forbidden fruit of the Tree of Knowledge they would die. They died out of the universal in the moment in which they were born into the individual. It would seem that the only means by which man may recover his unity with God is by giving up his separateness, his individual will. This does in fact occur in the mystic experience of the soul that we call 'conversion." In other words, to regain his aboriginal unity with God, man must die as a self-willing soul and be born again into the oneness of God.

God is obviously not a dictionary-defined and limited being, as here conceived, but being itself. Melville's point is that so long as man looks out from his individuality to see God, God is necessarily seen as an individuality like himself. If it were possible to draw God into the self, then both the self and God might lose all limitation; thus man might dwell in heaven and God would be found in the street. To put it somewhat differently, if a man could live always as man, the generic ideal, the universal rather than the particular man, then he would have succeeded in drawing God into himself.

In Melville's great epic novel, *Moby Dick*, there is a paragraph which illustrates the God-like universal quality of man. Melville is speaking of Starbuck, the first mate of the whaling ship *Pequod:*

But were the coming narrative to reveal, in any instance, the complete abasement of poor Starbuck's fortitude, scarce might I have the heart to write it; for it is a thing most sorrowful, nay shocking, to expose the fall of valor in the soul. Men may seem detestable as joint stock-companies and nations; knaves, fools, and murderers there may be; men may have mean and meagre faces; but man, in the ideal, is so noble and so sparkling, such a grand and glowing creature, that over any ignominious blemish in him all his fellows run to throw their costliest robes. That immaculate manliness we feel within ourselves, so far within us, that it remains intact though all

the outer character seem gone; bleeds with keenest an-
guish at the undraped spectacle of a valor-ruined man.
Nor can piety itself, at such a shameful sight, completely
stifle her upbraidings against the permitting stars. But
this august dignity I treat of, is not the dignity of kings
and robes, but that abounding dignity which has no
robed investiture. Thou shalt see it shining in the arm that
wields a pick or drives a spike; that democratic dignity
which, on all hands, radiates without end from God!
Himself! The great God absolute! The centre and cir-
cumference of all democracy! His omnipresence, our di-
vine equality.

Except for differences of style, this eloquent tribute
to the dignity of the human soul and to the ideal man that
exists potentially in every real man, no matter how humble, might have been written by Emerson or Whitman.
It shows beyond question that Melville was not, at this
time, without faith in the possibility of a democratic society. On this point of equality I should like to quote from
another letter of Melville's, written to Hawthorne in
June, 1851, in which he says, referring to a passage in his
letter on God: "You perceive I employ a capital initial
in the pronoun referring to the Deity; don't you think
there is a slight dash of flunkeyism in that usage?" Further in the same letter he writes: "With no son of man do
I stand upon any etiquette or ceremony, except the Christian ones of charity and honesty. . . . So, when you see or
hear of my ruthless democracy on all sides you may possibly feel a touch of a shrink, or something of that sort.
It is but nature to be shy of a mortal who boldly declares
that a thief in jail is as honorable a personage as Gen.

George Washington." In still another letter to Hawthorne, written in November, 1851, he exclaims: "Lord, when shall we be done growing? As long as we have anything more to do, we have done nothing." But all these letters were written during the year in which he created his masterpiece, when his powers were at their peak and when his faith in himself and in man was still strong.

The theme of *Moby Dick* is Captain Ahab's insane determination to find and destroy the white whale, which became for him the embodiment of all that opposes, baffles, and finally defeats the human will and the human intellect. Ahab's error was the error of Hawthorne's scientist in "The Birthmark" and of Dr. Rappaccini also; it was the error of Lucifer in *Paradise Lost,* who thought that he was greater than the All-Highest; it is the error of every man whose individual will swells to such proportions that he imagines that it can oppose the absolute will of the universe. Ahab is destroyed by the whale, but like Lucifer he remains defiant in his defeat. I do not identify Ahab with Melville, although Melville may have pictured in the grim captain a kind of insanity which he sometimes feared for himself. It is more probable that he used each of his characters to embody a quality of human nature, and that we shall find the author in no one of them.

Melville could not understand the mystic experience by which the transcendentalists claimed to have communication with God. In the novel *Pierre,* which was written next after *Moby Dick,* he said: "That profound Silence, that only Voice of our God, which I before spoke of; from that divine thing without a name, those imposter philosophers pretend somehow to have got an answer; which is as absurd, as though they should say they had got water out of a stone, for how can a man get a Voice out of Silence?" We cannot hope, then, to understand God. He seems to have come to the conclusion that the same is true of the soul of man, for he writes: "He [Pierre] saw that human life doth truly come from that which all men are agreed to call by the name of *God*; and that it partakes of the unravelable inscrutableness of God." Let a man beware of rashly exploring the shoreless seas of his own being. "Appalling is the soul of a man! Better might one be pushed off into the material spaces beyond the uttermost orbit of our sun, than once feel himself fairly afloat in himself!"

In all this Melville agreed with the transcendentalists except on one important point. They believed that the soul, whether of God or man, can be known by intuition, and that this knowledge transcends the limitations of fate. The evidence of this knowledge is present in the moral sense. Melville denied that the soul can be known, and pointed out the danger of seeking knowledge of it, yet could not altogether resist the temptation himself. He scorned intuition which could know spirit only in terms of spirit, caring only for that knowledge which can translate the soul's mysteries in terms of the intellect. This, too, was the evil that beset Ahab. If Ahab had been content to find his satisfactions in the spirit, he would have won his victory over Moby Dick, the white whale, without ever lowering a boat for him. Although Melville may have understood this truth as a law of spirit, he was infected with Ahab's desire to find a satisfaction in personal victories which he knew, finally, he could not gain. The effect was to throw him back into a state of skepticism and pessimism, which shows itself in his next book, *The Con-*

fidence Man, in a lack of faith in human nature. Melville thus stands midway between the faith of the transcendentalists and the extreme pessimism and determinism that developed in American thought a generation or two later.

Having examined several of Emerson's contemporaries whose idealisms were avowed with qualifications of one kind or another, let us turn now to one whose faith in nature and in the self-sufficiency of his own soul was complete and unwavering. This was Henry David Thoreau, born in Concord in 1817, neighbor of Emerson and friend of all honest beings from woodchucks to Hindu deities. At first he was a disciple of Emerson, but he presently learned to think for himself. He was a graduate of Harvard College, land surveyor, maker of pencils, handy man in Emerson's household, dweller in the woods, and author of two books published in his lifetime and of several collected and issued after his death.

"There is in my nature, methinks," he wrote in his first book, *A Week on the Concord and Merrimack Rivers,* "a singular yearning toward all wildness." This is perhaps the reason for his passion for nature, where individualism is the law of life. In the same book he wrote: "The wisest man preaches no doctrines: he has no scheme; he sees no rafter, not even a cobweb, against the heavens." The wise man reveals truth, which is not a doctrine or a scheme; he can reveal truth because he looks directly, not through some limiting medium, into the universal mind, here symbolized by the cloudless sky. Further he writes: "In my short experience of human life, the *outward* obstacles, if there were such, have not been living men, but the institutions of the dead. . . . Men execute nothing so faithfully as the wills of the dead, to the last codicil and letter. *They* rule this world, and the living are but their executors." Thoreau would remove the will of the past surviving as the institutions of the present which come between men, and permit them to deal with one another face to face as free individuals, just as the wise man deals with the universal, that is, God, face to face. Institutions restrict the freedom of the individual and warp his growth.

Thoreau's idealism is allegorically represented in the following passage from his second and greatest book, *Walden:*

> *I long ago lost a hound, a bay horse, and a turtle-dove, and am still on their trail. Many are the travellers I have spoken concerning them, describing their tracks and what calls they answered to. I have met one or two who had heard the hound, and the tramp of the horse, and even seen the dove disappear behind a cloud, and they seemed as anxious to recover them as if they had lost them themselves.*

In this little fable Thoreau suggests the immemorial and not uncommon human experience in which the individual soul is made vaguely aware of its origin and its destination in God. It is the transcendental idealist's vision of what in Christian theology is called the fall of man and his final redemption. It is what Wordsworth described in his great ode as "intimations of immortality." When the intimations become so strong that they have the validity of sensuous experience, we call them mystical revelations. Probably every person has this experience in some degree in the course of a lifetime, though often, as in the case of Poe, it is assumed to be an aesthetic rather than a religious experience. In either case it is man's obscure image of the soul's perfection in God; it is the ideal.

Thoreau is sometimes laughed at because, as it is supposed, he advocated living in a shanty in the woods as a cure for the evils of industrialism. This is ridiculous. "I went to the woods," he says, "because I wanted to live deliberately, to front only the essential facts of life . . . to drive life into a corner, and reduce it to its lowest terms, and, if it proved to be mean, why then to get the whole and genuine meanness of it, and publish its meanness to the world; or if it were sublime, to know it by experience, and be able to give a true account of it in my next excursion." After two years he left the shanty by Walden Pond, and this is what he wrote:

I left the woods for as good a reason as I went there. . . . I learned this, at least, by my experiment: that if one advances confidently in the direction of his dreams, and endeavors to live the life which he has imagined, he will meet with a success unexpected in common hours. He will put some things behind, will pass an invisible boundary; new, universal, and more liberal laws will begin to establish themselves around and within him; or the old laws be expanded, and interpreted in his favor in a more liberal sense, and he will live with the license of a higher order of beings. In proportion as he simplifies his life, the laws of the universe will appear less complex, and solitude will not be solitude, nor poverty poverty, nor weakness weakness. If you have built castles in the air, your work need not be lost; that is where they should be. Now put the foundations under them.

Those who think of the transcendentalists as dreamers

unconcerned with the world of affairs should note carefully the last sentence of this quotation from *Walden*. Thoreau here informs his readers in unmistakable terms that, in his opinion, men should be idealists in conception and practical builders in execution. Most idealists will agree with him that there is no inconsistency in these two functions, but that, on the contrary, they are complementary and mutually helpful.

Next to *Walden*, Thoreau's most famous work is his essay on "Civil Disobedience." One example of its wide influence is Mohandas Gandhi's use of it in formulating his policy of passive resistance. There was a kind of compensation in this, for Thoreau studied the wisdom books of ancient India and had been somewhat influenced by them. He began his essay by accepting the motto, "That government is best which governs least," and then had further stated his belief that "that government is best which governs not at all." This is individualism carried to its utter extreme of anarchy, and he admitted that men were not yet prepared for such an ideal society, but he believed it not altogether beyond hope of achievement. Speaking more practically as a citizen, he asked, "not at once no government, but *at once* a better government." This better government would be one in which only questions of expediency are settled by majority opinion, whereas questions of right and wrong are referred to the individual conscience. We shall understand Thoreau better if we remember that he was here objecting to a specific and immediate evil, the Fugitive Slave Law. He was sure it was a bad law, and he insisted that it was his duty and the duty of every other honest person to oppose it by disobeying it, regardless of the consequences to himself. If a number of such persons should act together against the unjust law their action, although it should subject the actors to punishment by law, might lead to the repeal of the bad laws and the making of better ones. Such an objection must, of course, be justified by the individual's adherence to the moral law and not by mere personal advantage.

The greatest single contribution of Thoreau to American idealism was his uncompromising individualism, and the next greatest was his enthusiasm for nature—the woods and fields—as an antidote for too much urban civilization. We cannot trust ourselves to live by the moral law in defiance of statutes and courts, nor can we always escape the city and live in the woods. We sadly misunderstand him if we suppose that he intended such a thing. What he actually did was to write the individual's declaration of independence from society, and that is a fundamental document in the annals of American culture. What is more, he took away from nature the ancient curse of Adam and made it companionable. He is our most perfect example of man at home in nature. Others would come who could speak for organization and the values of industry and community life. Thoreau did not deny their right to speak nor the justice of their claims; but as for himself, he felt an imperative need to assert the freedom of man as an individual, at home in the fields and woods and consorting familiarly with the wild creatures that inhabit them.

Looking back over the course of American literature from Emerson's *Nature* to Thoreau's *Walden*, I am impressed with the thought that this rich harvest of creative imagination was the fruition of pent-up energies accumulating over a period of two hundred years. Along the Atlantic seaboard from Boston to Richmond, matter was being transmuted into mind and action sublimated into imagination; in short, a culture was ripening to decay. The spiritual genealogy of these writers extended back to remote times, and the rudeness of their pioneer forbears had been refined away. None of them, with the possible exception of Emerson, realized what further growth awaited their quickening ideas in the vast hinterland west of the Appalachian barrier. Nevertheless, this fruition bore the seeds of a new American culture which, let us hope, will be broader, richer, and more lasting than the original. The first full-voiced spokesman for this culture of the future, product of the old and linking it with the new, was the poet Walt Whitman, whose work will be the subject of the next chapter.

V

Whitman

In 1855 two books appeared which offer an interesting contrast. One was Longfellow's *Hiawatha*, a collection of myths about the "natural" man who inhabited North America before the coming of the Europeans. The other was Walt Whitman's *Leaves of Grass*, a collection of poems about the "natural" man of the future who, the poet believed, will become the ideal and pattern of American democracy. *Hiawatha* was a best seller; *Leaves of Grass* sold not at all.

The first edition of *Leaves of Grass* was a thin quarto volume bound in green cloth stamped with gold. It had no name on the title page, but bore as frontispiece the portrait of the author in a characteristic pose. It contained one long poem and eleven shorter ones, none of which had titles. The book was designed, set up, and printed by Whitman himself on a press belonging to a friend who was a job printer. He sent copies to the literary journals, but there were only a few reviews and most of these were scathing in their criticism of the poems. He wrote several reviews himself and published them anonymously in friendly journals, trying in this way to secure for his book a few readers at least. Still it did not sell. He sent copies to important writers and critics, but they were mostly ignored. Emerson, however, was delighted with the book

79

and wrote Whitman an enthusiastic letter in which, among other complimentary things, he said: "I find it the most extraordinary piece of wit and wisdom that America has yet contributed. I am very happy in reading it, as great power makes us happy... I find incomparable things, said incomparably well, as they must be... I greet you at the beginning of a great career, which yet must have had a long foreground somewhere, for such a start."

Whitman was so greatly encouraged by Emerson's generous approval that neither the neglect nor the condemnation of the rest of the critics could seriously impair his confidence in his genius. In 1856 he issued a new edition of *Leaves of Grass* containing the original poems with some revisions and many new ones. Other editions were issued from time to time, always with the poems of the earlier issues revised and some new poems, so that in the last edition personally supervised by Whitman, published just before his death in 1892, the book contains close to four hundred separate titles.

Emerson recognized in *Leaves of Grass* the robust American manhood that he had been demanding from his countrymen for twenty years, and he probably guessed that his own lectures and writings were a part of the "long foreground" of Whitman's career as a poet. As a matter of fact many, perhaps most, of the ideas of *Leaves of Grass* can be found also in Emerson's essays and poems published before 1855, and it is reasonably certain that some of them were derived from that source. On the other hand, the same ideas, or a part of them, were available to any reader of Wordsworth, Coleridge, Carlyle, Goethe, the romantic and especially the transcendental poets and philosophers, and even the current English and American periodicals. The full extent of his reading we cannot know because he kept no systematic record of it and there is no correspondence surviving from this period. Besides, he consciously followed the advice given by Emerson in the address on "The American Scholar," and read to stimulate his own thinking rather than to store his mind with the thoughts of others. His learning was fragmentary and imperfect, and it is hard to separate what is original in his thinking from what is derivative. The only fact we can be sure of is that somehow before 1855 he had acquired a more or less intimate knowledge of the most important of the great poets, scientists, and philosophers of Europe and America.

His knowledge of geography was extraordinary. He studied geographies and atlases assiduously, and he was an eager questioner of travelers from strange lands. But his primary interest was in America and its wonders. He collected every scrap of information he could find about every state in the Union, whether it concerned topography, industry, or people. In this way, no doubt, he learned much of the frontier. He also had personal knowledge of the West, gained during a trip to New Orleans in 1848 by way of the Ohio and Mississippi rivers. He was in New Orleans for three months, and the exotic character of this cosmopolitan city had a lasting effect upon his life.

He was active in politics during the eighteen-forties while he was engaged in newspaper work, for newspapers in those days were political organs. His connections were with the Democratic Party in New York, and of course he was indoctrinated with the principles of Jefferson. During this period he was naturally influenced by the western forthrightness of Andrew Jackson, and this further heightened his interest in the West. When Lincoln became the leader of the Republican Party he affiliated himself with that, and during the Civil War became a great admirer of Lincoln as the embodiment of the democratic spirit in America. He was born on a farm on Long Island, of English, Welsh, and Dutch ancestry, and he had grown up and lived his young manhood in New York and its environs; hence he might with some justice claim to be a representative American and to speak as the poet of democracy.

In the first thirteen lines of his first poem, "Song of Myself," he states both his purpose and his qualifications to fulfill that purpose. These lines are worth quoting because they contain the gist of Whitman's meaning:

I celebrate myself, and sing myself,
And what I assume you shall assume,
For every atom belonging to me as good belongs to you.

I loafe and invite my soul,
I lean and loafe at my ease observing a spear of summer
    grass.

My tongue, every atom of my blood, form'd from this
    soil, this air,
Born here of parents born here from parents the same, and
    their parents the same,
I, now thirty-seven years old in perfect health begin,
Hoping to cease not till death.

Creeds and schools in abeyance,
Retiring back a while sufficed at what they are, but never
    forgotten,

*I harbor for good or bad, I permit to speak at every
        hazard,
Nature without check with original energy.*

But the Poet of Democracy is not always as clear and simple as he is in these lines. He was a mystic who believed that the deepest truths lie beyond the power of the understanding but are revealed dimly through intuition. These deeper truths cannot be definitely and clearly expressed by the poet to whom they are revealed because they are not definite or clear to him. They must be suggested, hinted, as he preferred to say, and conveyed indirectly by symbols. The same symbols recur so often, however, that it is possible from a careful study of all the poems to determine his meanings with considerable accuracy. Without going into detail, for it is a subject of considerable complication, I shall state as briefly as I can for the purposes of this essay what Whitman appeared to believe concerning the concepts of God, nature, man, the state, and democracy.

For the sake of perspective it may be well to recall Emerson's concept of the universe as a unity in duality, the fundamental duality being that of spirit and matter. Everything conceivable exists in relation to something else which is its opposite and has its full meaning only in that relationship. This is what he called the polarity of nature. There are, then, the thing and its opposite and their relationship, which together constitute a trinity. The third factor, the relationship, is the unifying principle. This trinitarian unity obviously resembles the Biblical Trinity of Father, Son, and Holy Ghost, particularly if the Father be interpreted as spirit, the Son as the realization of spirit in matter, and the Holy Ghost as the active principle or meaning that binds the two into one. The German philosopher Hegel conceived the Father as abstract idea, the Son as nature, and the Holy Ghost as the church. This basic metaphor of the trinity is almost everywhere used as a key to the mystery of being, in pagan as well as in Christian lands.

Whitman's concept of the universal being is represented by a square or four-sided figure instead of the conventional three-sided figure. The concept is explained in a poem published just after the Civil War entitled "Chanting the Square Deific." The poem consists of four sections, each describing one side of the square and personifying it. The four sides together constitute the One, or unity, and the differences appear from changes in the point of view. The first side described is that of law, including both the law of moral judgments and the law of physical nature. This side he personifies as Jehovah, or, in terms of other religions, Brahma and Saturn, and represents it as the Father. The second side is that of love, and it is personified as Christ, Hermes, or Hercules, involving the functions of consolator, messenger, and helper. The third side is the side of pride and revolt, personified as Satan, and involving the idea of the outcast and the evil as well as that of the free and independent individual. The fourth side is personified as "Santa Spirita," a term which appears to have originated with Whitman, by which he means the general soul or life of the universal being—the creative and unifying principle.

Although Whitman indicated corresponding personifications from pagan religions, all four of these aspects of deity have their most perfect correspondence in Christian theology. Jehovah, Christ, and Satan we know, of course, and Santa Spirita is merely a new name for the Holy Ghost, which is the life-giving presence of God remaining in the world after Christ's ascension, and which was represented by Milton in *Paradise Lost* to have created the world. But Whitman is unorthodox in including Satan in the godhead with the other three. Jehovah is the stern father who rules with impartial justice; Christ is the gentle son who longs to give all and receive nothing, to take all penalties and all suffering upon himself, and to offer mercy in place of the father's justice; Satan is the proud, selfish, disobedient son, resentful of the authority of the father and unfriendly towards his brother Christ; Santa Spirita is the mother in whose all-pervading life the other three subsist as one effective being. Whitman does not specifically state that Santa Spirita is feminine, but the form of the words might so indicate. However, the significance of the term is the same, whether masculine or feminine, and indeed it is possible that the question of sex is not involved at all. Jehovah is the immutable structure of law, by virtue of which all effects proceed infallibly from their necessary causes; Santa Spirita is the creative principle, the unseen life, that animates the structure of law; Christ and Satan are the opposite poles of that life as perceived in the human world. What Satan denies, Christ affirms; what Satan disjoins, Christ reunites; and what Satan entices to self-assertion and death, Christ leads to self-denial and redemption. This is the "Square Deific," which was Whitman's conception of the universal being.

Whitman agreed with Emerson that physical nature is the incarnation of the universal being in the realm of the unconscious. Jehovah is present there as natural law, and Christ and Satan are represented in the polarity of matter; that is, in action and reaction, attraction and repulsion, and similar pairs of opposites. It is reasonable to question whether, in what we call inanimate matter, Santa Spirita, the soul, is at all present; but Whitman believed that it is present. In one of his first poems, "To Think of Time," he exclaims:

> *I swear I think now that every thing without*
> *exception has an eternal soul!*
>
> .   .   .   .   .
>
> *I swear I think there is nothing but immortality!*

The soul, in non-living matter as in living matter, is the unifying principle, but in the former it is unconscious and inorganic and therefore completely determined. There is no disharmony of the individual will in opposition to the will of God. But the conflict within nature goes on nevertheless, and we can study its processes in the sciences of geology, physics, and chemistry. As the soul grows towards consciousness in plant life and the lower forms of animal life we can study the processes of change in the biological sciences. The theory of evolution is the consequence of man's effort to follow and explain the course of this development through conflict. Whitman was not acquainted with the Darwinian theory of evolution when the poems printed in the first three editions of *Leaves of Grass* were composed, but he fully subscribed to the theory of evolution which prevailed at that time. This theory supposed evolution to be the effect of some purposeful cause in nature rather than of what Darwin termed "natural selection." Whitman was much influ-

enced by the Hegelian theory of evolution through an
endlessly repeated and universal process of conflict and
reconciliation of opposites in accordance with the logical
formula: thesis, antithesis, synthesis. No sooner is a given
conflict reconciled than another is commenced on a higher
plane of being. In his "Song of the Open Road" Whitman said that "it is provided in the essence of things that
from any fruition of success, no matter what, shall come
forth something to make a greater struggle necessary."
By "fruition of success" he means any synthesis of oppos-
ing forces, whether they be conscious or unconscious.

As the physical world is the incarnation of the universal being in the realm of the unconscious, rising through
the intermediate stage of plant life into the realm of consciousness in the life of animals, so the human world,
which has developed the moral law, is an incarnation of
the universal being in the realm of the self-conscious. The
individual human being is therefore a complete microcosm manifesting the four-fold unity attributed by Whitman to the universal being. In fact, every individual identity, whether in physical nature, in the world of living
things, or in the realm of human creations, reflects the
four-fold structure of the whole, and whatever is true of
one must be true of the other. The universe, the earth,
man, the living cell, the state, the poem—they are all
identities made on the same principle. Santa Spirita, the
soul, gives life to all, even though the life of inanimate
nature is still latent. Hence it is that in the poem "Kos-
mos" he describes the cosmic man as one who

> out of the theory of the earth and of his or
> her body understands by subtle analogies all other
> theories,

*The theory of a city, a poem, and of the large politics of
these States;*

Individual man stands central in creation because he is the
masterpiece of creation, the fullest incarnation of the deific being. In him Jehovah is the physical and moral law,
Satan is egotism or pride, and Christ is altruism or love.
Santa Spirita, as always, is the unifying soul; and the soul
is the same whether in the individual or in the universal.
The whole of primary creation comes to a focus in man,
and from him flows a secondary creation, the products of
the finite mind. It is true, then, as Whitman says in "By
Blue Ontario's Shore," that "the whole theory of the universe is directed to one single individual—namely to
You." Again in the same poem he declares, "Produce
great persons, the rest follows."

These great persons are what Emerson called men of
character. Both Emerson and Whitman, therefore, agreed
that the individual is more than the state, as he must be
because he is its creator, even as God, the creator of man,
is greater than man. But if the creator of the state is great,
the state will also be great. The difficulty is that the state
is the creation of many men, some of whom are great, perhaps, but certainly not all. Besides this, the conflicting
forces within the state are not inherent. The entire system
is a fabrication of the mind, or of many minds, and not an
organic growth. But unless the structure of the state can
be made to conform to the pattern of the universal and the
individual—that is, unless it is, like a natural organism,
self-consistent and self-determined—the free development of the human race will not be possible. Although
the institution is the creation of man, once created it be-

comes a limitation upon his freedom. Abstractly considered, the state is composed of the following phases, corresponding to the four phases of the divine square: the
sovereign, who is the source of law; the subjects, who, in
their natural desire for individual freedom, are the enemies of the sovereign; the spirit of love or co-operation
that draws these two together in some compromise between rigid law and irresistible freedom; and the spirit
of nationality which unites and is the life of the state.
Here roughly are the four persons of the square deific:
Jehovah, law; Satan, individual freedom; Christ, brotherhood and co-operation; and Santa Spirita, nationality.

In the older forms of the state, the monarchy and the
oligarchy, the sovereign was entirely separated from most
of the subjects by class divisions, and the two groups con-
stituted antithetical members in the body of the state.
This fundamental difference made it impossible for them
to be reconciled, for while one class had both rights and
duties, the other had only duties. The principle of love
was frustrated for two reasons: first because love is effective only when the contestants are equal, and second because the two classes of subjects—for of course members
of the upper class were subjects as well as sovereign—had
different ideals of freedom, with the result that co-operation was possible only within the upper class. This left the
lower class little hope for the mitigation of law. The consequent intensification of strife between the sovereign and
the lower class of subjects, who were in the majority, inevitably disrupted the state, vitiated the national spirit,
and blocked the path of progress.

By avoiding this division into classes, the democratic
state attains something like organic unity. Its sovereign

and its subjects are the same, to wit, the whole people; hence both conflict and reconciliation take place within a single group. But one may ask, as Thoreau did, how the individual is free if he is subjected to the sovereign will of a majority of the whole body of citizens. Whitman's theory of democracy assumes that not only does sovereignty reside in the whole people, but it also resides in each individual, because each individual is free and without any superior; because he is self-determined and supreme. Whitman's theory of multiple "supremes" is stated in these lines from "By Blue Ontario's Shore":

Have you thought there could be but a single supreme?
There can be any number of supremes—one does not
countervail another any more than one eyesight
countervails another, or one life countervails an-
other.

The supremacy of each implies the equality of all; for if all were not equal, some would certainly be less than supreme, in which case they could not be free. Whitman's democracy, then, is made up of free individuals, each supreme and all equal. This theory is not such a paradox as it may seem at first, for, as we have seen, the individual is a being of four phases, of which only one, Satan, leads him to assert the freedom of the self and the dominance of the individual will. Another phase, equally powerful at least, leads him to forego his own will and fulfill the will of the whole or of any other individual. To obey the impulse to forego my own will and fulfill the will of another is not a limitation of my freedom and does not impair my sovereignty. This inherent power of the individual to sacrifice the self for the benefit of another or of the group is the basis of all human co-operation. We must believe that it is inherent in human nature or else give up all hope of establishing a permanent and successful democratic society. To liberty, or freedom, and equality, we must consequently add fraternity before we can have the fulfillment of our democratic dream.

When Whitman arranged his poems he did not follow a chronological order, but a thematic order. He put first the poems of a general nature, which he called "Inscriptions." The very first poem begins with these two lines:

One's-Self I sing, a simple separate person;
Yet utter the word Democratic, the word En-Masse.

I suspect he wanted these lines to appear first in his book because they state at once the fundamental doctrine of all his teaching. The individual is sacred and must maintain his separateness; but the group is necessary and must also be maintained. Somehow the two must be reconciled, or synthesized, and it is precisely in the synthesis that progress is achieved. In a patriotic poem entitled "Thou Mother with Thy Equal Brood" Whitman describes his vision of America in a metaphor somewhat like the square deific, although different in the naming of the four elements:

Lo, where arise three peerless stars,
To be thy natal stars my country, Ensemble,
         Evolution, Freedom,
Set in the sky of Law.

It is obvious that by "Ensemble" he means the interest of the whole co-operatively secured, and that by "Freedom" he means the maintenance of individual rights. "Evolution" suggests the process of development through compromise between the individual and the group and between individuals. "Law" is, of course, the constitutions and statutes within which the individual and the government must operate. We can identify Law with Jehovah, and Freedom with Satan, and perhaps we can also identify Ensemble with Christ and Evolution with Santa Spirita. From the comparison of this figure with the square deific two significant facts appear. First, since constitutions and statutes exist for the protection as well as the limitation of the freedom of the individual, Jehovah is revealed not only as the check upon the willfulness of Satan but also as the guarantor of his rights. Second, since Evolution may be identified with Santa Spirita, which in the organism of the state has been interpreted as the spirit of nationality, the fusion of the individual will with the will of the community must be understood not only as an evidence of patriotism but likewise as a means to social progress. There is this difference in the structure of the two figures, that in the square deific Santa Spirita (equated with Evolution) is the encloser, whereas in the other figure Law appears to be the encloser. However, the general sense is the same either way, to wit, that the state, like the universal being and like the individual man, is a synthesis of conflicting powers.

The four-fold action prevails whether the opposition is between the individual and any group, such as city, state, or nation, or between the national government and some component of government. It prevails also if the conflict is between two individuals within a group or two smaller groups within a larger group. In every case power and growth come from a right combination of resistance and co-operation within a firm but not absolutely rigid framework. All of this is a philosophical justification of the system of government with which we are familiar in the United States.

Whitman was not content that men should be politically free and in all else enslaved; that would leave to them the mere husk of democracy. There is no real democracy unless it pervades the whole structure of society. He was therefore the inveterate foe of economic privilege of every kind and a passionate defender of the opinion that the material benefits of civilization belong to all the people. How these benefits should be distributed he wisely refrained from saying, for he was not technically qualified to speak, and he no doubt realized that methods would vary from time to time.

In their social intercourse a democratic people should be natural and sincere, but not crude or immoral. If in his poems Whitman is occasionally boisterous, he is only protesting against the smug decorum of a conventionalized society. No poet ever advocated a healthier and loftier morality than he. If he tried to lift sex out of its degradation and liberate it from taboos, it was because he believed it to be the most spiritual part of man's nature, the physical counterpart of the divine creative mind, and an integral part of the soul. If he professed to be the poet of evil as well as of good and to be himself as evil as any, it was because he was convinced that evil is only the spirit of freedom overleaping its divine function, and that without evil, or that which produces evil, there can be no good. And if he exalted pride, which is the original evil because it is the original assertion of freedom in the self, he also exalted love, which is the ultimate good because it is the ultimate renunciation of the self. Within these extremes is embraced the whole gamut of morality.

Religion and art are also to become finally free in the democratic society. The democratic individual acknowledges no God except what waits intrinsically in himself, and that which waits is but man perfected. For him pride is no less sacred than love, and one must not be abased before the other. Thus Whitman, the type of the democratic individual, was not a complete mystic. Much as he exalted love, he did not believe in the complete renunciation of the self. The fellowship of equals is the highest expression of love in a democracy. The soul is assured of immortality, but it can carry into its existence in other spheres only what has accrued to it through the life of the body between birth and death. In a universe where all things are equally marvellous, the supernatural is absorbed in the natural. Man has no God, no Saviour, except himself at his best; he has no church and no bibles save those of his own making; yet Satan is real and ever active, and he is not without in some remote hell on God's sufferance, but within, an indispensable part of God himself. In a democracy, therefore, not less but more religion is needed; indeed, without a robust faith in humanity and a profound religious conviction of the goodness of the universe and of its unvarying progress towards divine perfection, it is hard to believe that a democratic society can long endure even if once established.

The introduction of democratic values into the aristocratic realm of art involves a revolution of considerable violence; for as judged by these values, all materials are equally susceptible of artistic treatment, and there is no law to govern the great artist except that which is inherent in the nature of the materials themselves and in himself. In his insistence upon fidelity to nature Whitman was a realist. Since the emphasis, as in the realm of politics, is upon the individual more than upon the group, it may appear to the casual observer that among all the realistic details there is no underlying principle of unity. Nevertheless, democratic art, as Whitman understood it, is not chaotic. It attempts to reproduce in the creations of the human mind the same organic unity of structure that characterizes the creations of the universal mind. The larger the design, the more prominent will be the individual parts and the more difficult the perception of unity. In *Leaves of Grass,* for example, which is an excellent model of democratic art, and which should be treated rather as a single great poem than as a collection of poems, the design is that of an "orbic," developing personality, to wit, the poet himself, that expands to the proportions of the universal without losing its individuality.

The democratic society of which Whitman dreamed can be realized only through the development of a type of individuality far superior to that of his own day or ours. Such development is not impossible if, as he believed, man is capable of infinite improvement. For if all are potentially perfect, then all are potentially equal. Successful democracy depends, not indeed upon actual equality, but upon the maintenance of a fluid condition of society in which the tendency is to lessen the gap between the advanced and backward groups and in which every effort is made to promote the individual instead of fixing his station at a given level. It is further necessary that material wealth shall not be the chief measure of success. To hasten

this development Whitman proposed a crusade of inten-
sive education, not primarily through the schools, but
through a high religious literature of which *Leaves of
Grass* should be the herald and example. He hoped that
inspired poets would arise who would carry forward the
work of evangelization begun by him and so, through the
cultivation of the emotions and the religious sense, pre-
pare the masses for that democratic society in which all
are to be equal and free and all inseparably united in the
universal sentiment of love and brotherhood.

VI

The Decline of Idealism

O NE OF THE DISCOURAGING
facts about progress is that it does not continue steadily in
a straight line, but curves and twists and turns back upon
itself like the channel of a great river. In the perspective
of a thousand years the course of human life is seen to flow
in the same general direction, but within the lifetime of a
single individual it may be, and sometimes is, following
a retrograde course. The cause of this reversal in the direction of human evolution is the same as that which changes
the current of the river; the stream meets an obstacle
which stops its forward movement and turns it aside until
some new channel can be found or made by which it can
resume its interrupted progress. It is only a fair-weather
optimist, therefore, who loses his faith in human progress
when he observes its course obstructed and reversed. The
farsighted optimist is likely to perceive in this temporary
setback the prelude to some momentous change which
will restore the forward movement of mankind and enable
it to develop in some new and unforeseen direction.

This may prove to be the significance of the decline of
idealism which began in America about the middle of the
last century. Emerson and his contemporaries had under-
estimated and perhaps misunderstood the materialism
that was already rising like a tide throughout the country,

in New England as well as in the great cities and over the teeming plains of the middle regions. This materialism was not a new thing; it had, like moral idealism, existed from the beginning in the character and circumstances of the colonial American. The causes of its rapid increase in the nineteenth century were manifold, but three of them were of such importance as to merit special mention. These were the Darwinian theory of evolution, the Civil War, and the emergence of the frontier spirit as a dominant force in business and politics.

Darwin's new theory of evolution by natural selection, announced in 1859, threatened men's belief, as older theories of evolution had not, in a universe created from design and developing by rational processes to a preconceived and desirable end. All the forces of religious orthodoxy bitterly attacked the new theory; moreover, the most reputable scientists of the day were arrayed against it, including Agassiz and Asa Gray at Harvard, James Dwight Dana at Yale, and James McCosh at Princeton. These scientists differed on many problems raised by the Darwinians, but they all agreed that the cherished belief in a designed and progressive evolution must be saved at all costs. Needless to say, the average layman was willing to accept their explanations and save his faith, and eventually interpreters learned to make the new kind of evolution sound like the familiar Emersonian brand. Of these popularizers perhaps the most successful was John Fiske. Late in the century and near the end of his life, he summed up his argument in a book that bore the comforting title, *Through Nature to God.* A single sentence from this book will indicate the nature of Fiske's conclusions: "The moral sentiments, the moral law, devotion to unselfish ends, disinterested love, nobility of soul—these are Nature's most highly wrought products, latest in coming to maturity; they are the consummation, toward which all earlier prophecy has pointed." Thus Fiske, while calling himself a Darwinian, really preached the moral idealism of Emerson.

Nevertheless, in subtle ways, the infection spread. The very attempt to gloss over the ugly features of Darwinism served to make it acceptable where otherwise it would have been carefully shunned. Unscrupulous men in business and politics made the new conception of life the justification for acts which their consciences would otherwise have repudiated, and so materialism gained ground by using the shibboleths of the old idealism.

More immediate in its effects was the Civil War. But even the war was fought, or was supposed by the participants to have been fought, for ideals. I think we may grant, with whatever reservations, that it was, and that those ideals could not have been attained by any other means then known to the people of the United States. It is the custom of many high-minded people to deny that any good can come of war; and I am myself emotionally disposed to agree with them, because their judgment, if true, promises that human wisdom and justice will eventually abolish this most inhuman of human institutions. A candid study of history will reveal the unpleasant fact, however, that men have never in the past proved capable of solving their most knotty problems except by recourse to war. By bitter wars men in the western world won religious freedom in the sixteenth and seventeenth centuries; by other wars in the eighteenth and nineteenth centuries they won political freedom; and it may be that only wars, and perhaps the bitterest of all, can settle the problem of economic freedom in this century and the next.

Wars often mark the passing of an old way of life and the coming of a new way. They are death throes and birth pangs, and men must grow much wiser than they now are before they can hope to escape these penalties under the law of change. The people of the United States have passed through two epoch-making wars in their brief history: the American Revolution and the Civil War. The Revolution was fought for political freedom, and its effect was the incorporation in the constitution and laws of this country of some of the ideals of the eighteenth century. The Civil War was fought to complete the work which the Revolution left incomplete, and among its effects were the abolition of negro slavery and the establishment of a strong Federal Union. The American Revolution, together with the French Revolution which followed soon afterward, marked the end of the age of rational idealism; the Civil War marked the end of the age of romantic idealism in America.

Terrible as it was in itself, the war was even more terrible in its moral effects. The good that was to come of the struggle did not immediately appear, but the evil was everywhere manifest. The powers of government and business were seized by unprincipled men and bigoted partisans, who proceeded to exploit the entire country for selfish ends. The southern states were left to the tender mercies of adventurers, opportunists, misguided reformers, and plain rascals, not all of whom, alas, were Yankees. Throughout the North and West also there was widespread corruption in politics and fraud in business, some of which began before the war was over and some of which continued for twenty-five years afterwards. The worst of this public and private thievery was exposed during the presidency of General Grant and rocked the country to its foundations, but the rascals had such a hold on the government that they were not easily shaken off.

Even Whitman, despite his robust optimism, was appalled. Between 1867 and 1870 he prepared the prose essay published in 1871 as *Democratic Vistas*. This essay contains an extensive description of public and private corruption in America, from which I quote the following excerpt:

I say we had best look our times and lands searchingly in the face, like a physician diagnosing some deep disease. Never was there, perhaps, more hollowness at heart than at present, and here in the United States. Genuine belief seems to have left us. The underlying principles of the States are not honestly believ'd in, (for all this hectic glow, and these melo-dramatic screamings,) nor is humanity itself believ'd in. What penetrating eye does not everywhere see through the mask? The spectacle is appalling. We live in an atmosphere of hypocrisy throughout. . . . The depravity of the business classes of our country is not less than has been supposed, but infinitely greater. The official services of America, national, state, and municipal, in all their branches and departments, except the judiciary, are saturated in corruption, bribery, falsehood, mal-administration; and the judiciary is tainted. The great cities reek with respectable as much as non-respectable robbery and scoundrelism. In fashionable life, flippancy, tepid amours, weak infidelism, small aims, or no aims at all, only to kill time. In business, (this

*all-devouring modern word, business,) the one sole ob-
ject is, by any means, pecuniary gain. . . . True, indeed,
behind this fantastic farce, enacted on the visible stage of
society, solid things and stupendous labors are to be discover'd, existing crudely and going on in the background,
to advance and tell themselves in time. Yet the truths are
none the less terrible. I say that our New World democracy, however great a success in uplifting the masses out
of their sloughs, in materialistic development, products,
and in a certain highly-deceptive superficial popular intel-
lectuality, is, so far, an almost complete failure in its social
aspects, and in really grand religious, moral, literary,
and esthetic results. In vain do we march with unprece-
dented strides to empire so colossal, outvying the antique,
beyond Alexander's, beyond the proudest sway of Rome.
In vain have we annex'd Texas, California, Alaska, and
reach north for Canada and south for Cuba. It is as if we
were somehow being endow'd with a vast and more and
more thoroughly-appointed body, and then left with little or no soul.*

This collapse of idealism was not a consequence of the
Civil War exclusively, although a part of the price of war
has always been a following period of moral disintegra-
tion. The spread of Darwinian ideas, as I have already
stated, had a similar effect. A third cause, and an important
one, was the final and complete triumph of the frontier
spirit. Even in colonial times the frontier had been a refuge for social misfits and lawless elements as well as for
the authentic pioneer and builder, and so it continued to
be. The rigors of military dictatorship in wartime drove
new thousands into the plains and mountains, where every

man was a law unto himself. Here a rampant individualism developed and after the war spread back eastward until it infected the entire nation. Men were intoxicated with dreams of fabulous wealth and took advantage of the moral letdown following the war to twist the confused thoughts and emotions of the people into a fabric of materialistic philosophy that suited their own pecuniary aims. Between 1860 and 1890 the great West was all settled, the railroads built, industrialism established in the East, and capital organized and centered in the great cities of the Atlantic seaboard to which all the rest of the country was made tributary. In the face of industrial organization the labor unions were born, and in the 1880's there began the bitter conflict between capital and labor, with its strikes and lockouts and all the other troubles that the twentieth century has inherited without the power to remedy. And then we reached and filled the last frontier and discovered that at last we were left with all the evils of violence and greed that the frontier spirit had encouraged without the compensating benefits it had afforded. It was a familiar story in the history of human development. The spirit of man, represented by the courage and enterprise of the pioneer, had mastered the wild West but had become infected in the process with its own wildness. The builder was imprisoned by the edifice he built.

Whitman understood what was happening. He knew that material greatness was a necessary preparation for spiritual greatness and not in permanent opposition to it. Physical power will in time be transformed to spiritual power. The builder will use the strength developed in erecting the building to free himself from it. Prometheus is not forever chained to the rock, but eventually loosed to bestow new blessings upon mankind. For this reason Whitman in his philosophic moods welcomed the material aggrandizement of America. In 1855, in "Song of Myself," he had said,

> *I accept Reality and dare not question it,*
> *Materialism first and last imbuing.*

And in 1876, in his "Song of the Exposition," he spoke proudly of America's material progress and called industry "sacred." At the conclusion of this poem, however, he explains that he does not praise wealth for itself—"Think not our chant, our show, merely for products gross or lucre"—but rather does he dedicate it to the spiritual uses of the nation. Another passage from *Democratic Vistas* will illustrate Whitman's way of linking material progress with the growth of the soul. "I hail with joy," he wrote,

> *I hail with joy the oceanic, variegated, intense practical energy, the demand for facts, even the business materialism of the current age, our States. But wo to the age or land in which these things, movements, stopping at themselves, do not tend to ideas. As fuel to flame, and flame to the heavens, so must wealth, science, materialism—even this democracy of which we make so much— unerringly feed the highest mind, the soul.*

In this spiritualizing of material values the chief instrument, in Whitman's opinion, is to be literature, and particularly poetry. Following the passage quoted above from *Democratic Vistas* he continues thus:

And as the purport of objective Nature is doubtless folded, hidden, somewhere here—as somewhere here is what this globe and its manifold forms, and the light of day, and night's darkness, and life itself, with all its experiences, are for—it is here the great literature, especially verse, must get its inspiration and throbbing blood. Then may we attain to a poetry worthy the immortal soul of man, and which, while absorbing materials, and, in their own sense, the shows of Nature, will, above all, have, both directly and indirectly, a freeing, fluidizing, expanding, religious character, exulting with science, fructifying the moral elements, and stimulating aspirations, and meditations on the unknown.

To perform for the democratic society of the future the function performed for feudal society by the knights and religious orders, he dreamed of a band of "conscience-conserving, God-inculcating, inspired achievers, not only in literature, the greatest art, but achievers in all art—a new, undying order, dynasty, from age to age transmitted . . ." Without such an order of poets and artists America, he thinks, cannot achieve true greatness, but having them "she will understand herself, live nobly, nobly contribute, emanate, and, swinging, poised safely on herself, illumin'd and illuming, become a full-form'd world, and divine Mother not only for material but spiritual worlds, in ceaseless succession through time."

It is clear that Whitman fully accepted the physical expansion and materialism in business that characterized the life of the United States during the thirty years following the outbreak of the Civil War, and if he was appalled by the things that were happening, it was only because the lawlessness and greed of a few individuals in politics and industry threatened to stifle the spiritual and æsthetic life which might be expected under normal conditions to develop from the soil of material wealth. He felt that it was his function to issue the call and set the example for the class of artists who must spiritualize the material body of America. So far, he admitted, writing about 1880, democracy "has not yet had a single representative worthy of it anywhere upon the earth" in the sphere of art. Americans, he thought, are not only the "most materialistic and money-making people ever known," but the "most emotional, spiritualistic, and poetry-loving people also."He liked to think that great prophet-poets would arise in America, like those of ancient Judea but more passionate, who would lead the people away from their condition of shallowness, corruption, and cankerous materialism into a condition of moral and æsthetic health. "Meanwhile," he concludes, "democracy waits the coming of its bards in silence and in twilight—but 'tis the twilight of the dawn."

An examination of American literature during the thirty years following the Civil War, the period which has been aptly dubbed "the Gilded Age," will reveal the justice of Whitman's condemnation of it. Some of the older writers were still active and popular, especially Longfellow and Whittier, but they were valued for their sentiment more than for their more virile qualities. This love of sentiment and a growing love of dainty trivialities and superficial cleverness were catered to by the younger poets. Among these younger poets were Bayard Taylor, Thomas Bailey Aldrich, and Richard Watson Gilder, and in their train followed a host of lesser versifiers, now forgotten, including numerous thin-voiced "female poets," to use the term then current. Popular fiction had for many years before the war been a strong mixture of blood and tears, well represented by such sentimental masterpieces as Susan Warner's *Wide Wide World* and T. S. Arthur's *Ten Nights in a Bar-Room*. Harriet Beecher Stowe's *Uncle Tom's Cabin* was the culmination of fiction in this style, but it was not the last of it; on the contrary, Mrs. Stowe's success continued to set the fashion for sentimental and moralistic stories for a generation after the war. Typical of these were E. P. Roe's *Barriers Burned Away* (1872) and Lew Wallace's *Ben-Hur* (1880), the latter being perhaps the best of this kind. About this time, moreover, the era of the sensational dime novel and western thriller began, and lasted till the end of the century. It seemed as if American literature became more and more artificial and remote from real life. No wonder Whitman's faith was strained, for he witnessed the moral idealism of the first half of the century dissolved in childish sensationalism, platitudes, and sentimental drivel.

A few able writers stood out above the mob of scribblers, but most of them failed in one way or another to come to grips with the real problems of the country. Emily Dickinson, born in 1830, carried on the tradition of New England idealism in the retirement of her village home in western Massachusetts. But she was unknown to Whitman and to everyone else except a few neighbors and friends, for she would not allow her poems to be published. In these odd little poems the mischief of Puck and the wisdom of the sage are suffused with the sense of wonder that is the quality of immortal childhood. Although she was shy and seldom left her room, the wide world was her garden and God was her playfellow. In her poetry we are made to know the loveliness of death and the death-lessness of love. There was in her temperament something of the serenity of Emerson, the intensity of Thoreau, and the rebelliousness of Whitman; yet she was not a pattern of qualities but one single quality that suggested relation-ships while remaining unique and unanalyzable. She was beyond all else original and individual. She was at one with the transcendentalists in her faith in the power of the individual to meet all contingencies. Thus she wrote:

> *We never know how high we are*
> *Till we are called to rise;*
> *And then, if we are true to plan,*
> *Our statures touch the skies.*

It may have been a wise instinct that kept Emily Dickin-son from offering her poems to the Gilded Age; even when they were published, in 1890, four years after her death, they received scant notice. It was not until after the chastening experience of the first World War that Ameri-can readers were in the mood to accept her work or quali-fied to understand it. Little as she might have suspected such an outcome, however, she stands for us now as a link between the "Golden Day" of Emerson and Whitman and the new day of Frost and Robinson.

Meanwhile, from war-torn and reconstruction-har-ried Georgia, came Sidney Lanier, an ex-Confederate soldier, who struggled for twenty years against poverty and disease to establish a place for himself in the arts of music and poetry, but died in 1881, at the age of thirty-nine, with his work only half finished. He wrote narratives for boys, lectured on the novel and on Shakespeare at Johns Hopkins University, played the flute marvelously in the Peabody Symphony Orchestra, and composed poems when he could. Lanier's idealism was genuine and passionately maintained, but the world he imagined was rather a reconstruction of an idealized past than a creation for the future. Instead of being naïve, realistic, and democratic, it was pious, sentimental, and aristocratic. His ideal man was more like Tennyson's Sir Galahad than Whitman's caresser of life. He was painfully aware of Darwin and the Machine Age, but he longed for a science that would leave his religious faith unimpaired, and for an industrial order that would live by the code of Christian knighthood. Like Emerson and Whitman he wished to reconcile good and evil, free will and fate, and all the other dichotomies of human experience, but he wanted to do it by converting evil to good and fate to free will. As a matter of fact, it is doubtful whether Lanier seriously believed in the possibility of resolving these age-old antagonisms, but made a dream into which he escaped from the problem. Music offered him a perfect escape from these conflicts because it lifted him out of the world of diverse things into the world of harmonious beauty. In his poetic tribute to Beethoven he says:

> *I know not how, I care not why,*
> *Thy music brings this broil at ease,*
> *And melts my passion's mortal cry*
> *In satisfying symphonies.*

This is the ecstasy of the artist rather than the mystic's union with God. It is more akin to Poe's sentiment of

poesy than to Emerson's transcendentalism. To modern
ears Lanier's poetry, although often beautiful, sounds
archaic and quaint, like the medieval romances.

The story of Bret Harte, the first successful representative of the West in literature, was very different.
He was born and reared next door to New England, in
Albany, New York, and went to California at the age of
eighteen. In 1869 he became the first editor of the *Over-
land Monthly*, and in the second issue of this magazine
he published his first successful short story, "The Luck
of Roaring Camp." Soon afterwards appeared "The Outcasts of Poker Flat," "Tennessee's Partner," and the humorous poem "Plain Language from Truthful James,"
better known as "The Heathen Chinee." In less than
three years Bret Harte had completed the work by which
he is best known; intoxicated with his success, he went to
New York where, though he worked steadily, he produced nothing more of importance. Emerson saw him in
1872, and the conversation turned on a passage in Emerson's essay "Civilization," in which he attributed to the
moral idealism of the pioneer the fact that he so quickly
introduces into his log hut the piano, books, and other
evidences of culture. Harte remarked, "Do you know
that, on the contrary, it is vice that brings them in? It is
the gamblers who bring in the music to California. It is
the prostitute who brings in the New York fashions of
dress there, and so throughout." This incident illustrates
both the similarity and the difference between the moral
idealism of Emerson and his contemporaries and the sentimental idealism of Harte and others of the Gilded Age.
In "The Luck of Roaring Camp" the presence of an or-
phaned baby, born of a disreputable Indian woman, trans-

formed the lives of a hundred men in the mining camp
from long-established habits of cruelty and vice to prodi-
gies of gentleness and virtue. In "The Outcasts of Poker
Flat," a hardened gambler and two confirmed prosti-
tutes become noble and self-sacrificing when they find
themselves in the company of an innocent girl of fifteen.
This sentimental confusion of evil with good has been
partly responsible for the spread of vice and crime and
the laxity of courts of justice in this country. The irony of
it is that it springs, though perhaps from a mistaken interpretation, from Emerson's doctrine of "the good of evil
born." Whitman, who agreed with Emerson, pointed out
how dangerous this doctrine can be when corrupted by
sentiment and hazy thinking and translated into action.
It has many times become the aid and comfort of evil
doers.

Bret Harte was not a great writer, but he taught
American writers the value of local color. He was the first
of an increasing number of regionalists, including his fellow Californian Joaquin Miller, George Washington
Cable in New Orleans, Joel Chandler Harris in Georgia,
and Sarah Orne Jewett in New England, and in this capacity he made an original contribution to literary history;
but he was not a true interpreter of the frontier spirit, and
in fact was never really at home in the West, which was
almost as much a place of romance to him as it was to those
who saw it through his eyes.

Strictly speaking, the frontier produced no literature
of the first rank. Life there was too strenuous for those
moods of reminiscence and reflection which are the necessary seed beds of art. After the frontier was gone, however, or after the writer, having known and left it, looked

back upon it through the haze of time or distance, then it became an inexhaustible source of raw material for the imagination. So it was with Mark Twain, who, unlike Bret Harte, was a genuine product of the frontier and a true interpreter of the frontier spirit.

He was born in Missouri in 1835, and spent his childhood and early youth in a town on the banks of the Mississippi River, where sooner or later the pageant of America passed before his eyes, high and low, good and bad, East, West, and South. He was for a time a steamboat pilot between St. Louis and New Orleans, until the outbreak of the Civil War put an end to this trade. Afterwards he was for a brief period a volunteer soldier in the Confederate Army, but he found that life too unexciting and so abandoned it to wander through the mining camps of Nevada and on to San Francisco, where he wrote for newspapers and came under the influence of Bret Harte. Undoubtedly he knew the old West better than any American writer has ever known it before or since. He also knew the East and the Middle West, for he spent four years before the war as a journeyman printer in New York, Philadelphia, Cincinnati, and other cities in those regions. In 1867 he left California and went to the East again, where presently he married a cultivated woman and established a permanent residence in the staid Puritan city of Hartford, Connecticut. Here he benefited by the chastening influence of Charles Dudley Warner, who was his neighbor, and William Dean Howells, who was his literary adviser. He remained a Westerner, but his intellectual life was deepened and his literary style was improved by acquaintance with the culture of the American East and of Europe.

He was one of the few literary men who, like Whitman, saw and criticized the shallowness, effrontery, and
corruption of American public and private life during the
Gilded Age. In fact, it was Mark Twain who first called
it the Gilded Age, for in 1873, in collaboration with Warner, he published a novel with that title. Of their theme
the authors wrote ironically in the preface to the book:

*It will be seen that it deals with an entirely ideal state
of society; and the chief embarrassment of the writers
in this realm of the imagination has been the want of illus-
trative examples. In a State where there is no fever of
speculation, no inflamed desire for sudden wealth, where
the poor are all simple-minded and contented, and the
rich are all honest and generous, where society is in a condition of primitive purity and politics is the occupation of
only the capable and the patriotic, there are necessarily
no materials for such a history as we have constructed out
of an ideal commonwealth.*

This is probably the most hilarious satire ever seriously
conceived by the mind of man. The most remarkable thing
in it is the character of Colonel Beriah Sellers, whose get-
rich-quick schemes were innumerable, and whose generosity and hospitality with nothing in the bank or the cup-
board were inexhaustible. He was the spirit of the age in
all but its sinister aspects, and he is as likable, and doubtless as immortal, as Dickens's Mr. Micawber. Needless
to say, Colonel Sellers is the creation of Mark Twain, and
in many respects he is a self-portrait, for the satirist of the
Gilded Age was a product of that age in its frontier phase.
In the treasure hunting of Tom Sawyer, and in Mark

Twain's own treasure hunting in the mines of Nevada, the
projected trip to South America, and later speculative in-
vestments in the East, the essential quality of Colonel Sellers is illustrated. It may be, therefore, that Mark Twain
was not as fearful of the consequences of American cupid-
ity as Whitman, although it was the humorist's privilege
to make a joke of the most serious matter.

    Whatever deductions must be made from Mark
Twain's satire on the materialism of the Gilded Age, the
sincerity of his attacks on its sentimentality is beyond question. He hated its simpering and sniveling, and he hated
its self-abasement before Europe. Emerson had written
America's intellectual declaration of independence, but
the new generation had apparently abandoned the virtues
of democratic self-reliance and was secretly, and sometimes openly, working to import the aristocratic distinc-
tions of Europe and graft them upon the stem of Americanism. His first two important books, *Innocents Abroad*
(1869) and *Roughing It* (1872), were new declarations
of independence on behalf of unsophisticated Americans
like himself, and although he went too far and sometimes
became rowdy, his performance was timely and wholesome. He continued his attacks on sentimentality in almost
everything he wrote, but the next work in which he definitely connected his attack with things European and delivered it with equally devastating effect was *A Connecticut Yankee in King Arthur's Court* (1889), which may
have been provoked by Tennyson's *Idylls of the King*.
His purpose in this work was not so much to praise the
Yankee and his mechanical ingenuity as to ridicule the
pseudo-medievalism that had become popular in America.

    Mark Twain was not altogether free of sentimentality

himself, as we may observe in his essay "In Defense of Harriet Shelley," where he is guilty of the very sins of which he accuses Shelley's biographers. His sincere admiration of Joan of Arc is evidence that there were even some things medieval that he could accept like a devotee. He was a man of many contradictions, and he was governed more by his emotions than by his rational mind. In short, he was a representative American of his time, whether of East or West, and illustrated the faults as well as the virtues of his fellow countrymen. Like them he was a lover of plots and adventures, of wild exaggeration and practical jokes, of natural wonders and mechanical ingenuities; like them too he was ignorant, cynical, and crude, but withal naïvely sincere and magnanimous. He was a typical adolescent: that was the source of his charm and his weakness.

Such an adolescent he has immortalized in the character of Huckleberry Finn, a perfect example of the natural man before he has grown up, who is contrasted with the unnatural Tom Sawyer, an example of the bad effect of artificial culture. The only native American in fiction who might reasonably be compared with Huckleberry Finn is Cooper's Leatherstocking, and yet one is inclined to smile at the comparison. What would Leatherstocking have been like at Huck Finn's age? One thinks of the scout's sententiousness and strait-laced morality in contrast with Huck's directness and freedom and prefers the latter. Tom Sawyer and Huckleberry Finn were the two sides of Mark Twain's nature; the one half-civilized and always acting a part, the other unspoiled and lovable though not always a truth-teller and, alas, not always clean! Mark Twain washed regularly, I believe, but his language often had to be sent to the cleaner before it was thought fit to appear in public.

In his last years, as everyone knows, Mark Twain became a pessimist. It was almost inevitable that he should, because he built his life on surfaces, and when, as he grew old, the surfaces wore thin and cracked, he could see the abysmal hollowness within. In this as in everything else he was representative of his age. He accepted the pronouncements of nineteenth century science as final and imperishable truths, unable to foresee the possibility that science might eventually teach man more than surfaces and mechanics and the destruction of idols. He was assured, when he wrote *Huckleberry Finn,* that the natural man is a creature of dignity and honor, but in his old age he forgot Huck Finn and supposed that man is no more in essence than he appears to be in his commercial relations. His instincts were right when they led him to imagine Huckleberry Finn; his intellect led him astray in such pessimistic rationalizations as the story of the town of Hadleyburg, in which every citizen is a thief and a liar. I will not say that Mark Twain lost his faith in human nature; he literally threw it away. He was the greatest American writer of his generation, but he was not great enough to understand either himself or his country.

VII

From Realism to Naturalism

THE POLITICAL AND ECO-
nomic division between North and South was at last effectively bridged, and even the differences between East
and West rapidly disappeared as the country developed;
but there was another division in American life, a subtle
one of long standing which could not be treated objec-
tively, and which became wider as the century progressed.
This was the old dichotomy of idealism and materialism
which since the time of Edwards and Franklin had given
a dual aspect to the American character. Religion depends
upon idealism for its sustenance, as science upon materialism; consequently, science became dominant with the
spread of materialism in the United States, whereas with
the decline of idealism religion lost much of its moral
force and hardened into competitive sectarian organizations. Eventually literature, which had been the voice of
idealism in the first half of the century, was likewise
divided, with the result that poetry adhered to idealistic
modes of thought and feeling, while fiction increasingly
adopted materialistic modes. Because of this division in
modern American literature, it will be convenient here-
after to discuss poetry and fiction separately.

Formal philosophy, which by this time had become
dissociated from theology, undertook to mediate between

the conflicting tendencies in American life. At first, American philosophy was almost exclusively idealistic. W. T. Harris and his associates, constituting the St. Louis school, worked diligently to establish the German romantic philosophy, particularly the absolute idealism of Hegel, in the United States. In Emerson's old age Harris, with the collaboration of Alcott, Sanborn, and others, established the Concord School of Philosophy with the purpose, apparently, of grafting German idealism upon New England transcendentalism. It was too late. The seed of skepticism, which had lain dormant since the days of deism, had now sprouted, and the plant was growing apace.

Yet idealism was by no means ready to surrender. Out of California came perhaps the greatest romantic idealist that America produced after Emerson. This was Josiah Royce, professor of philosophy at Harvard, who did what he could to stem the tide of skepticism. He believed that the infinite is latent in the finite, the eternal in the temporal, the ideal in the real. What is to be is not predetermined by an objective will outside the human world, but evolves from the series of individual willed acts within that world. In every action there is a subject and object, a perceiver and a thing perceived; but there is also a third thing, the interpretation or ideal meaning, which constitutes a step forward from the known to the unknown, from the real to the ideal. To relate his philosophy more closely to the practical world, Royce went so far as to identify the Absolute with what he called "the Spirit of Community." Even this concession was not enough, and Royce remains the philosopher of poets and intellectuals and is hardly more than a name to others.

A much greater compromise was made by William

James, Royce's Harvard colleague and one of the original pragmatists. He was a believer in the value of the emotions and an enemy of pure intellectualism. For him the universe is an experiment, passing forever from old conclusions to new premises; neither the end, if there is to be an end, nor the beginning, if there was a beginning, can be known. Nothing is absolute; all is relative. The test of truth is experience; a thing is true if it works. If called upon to choose between optimism and pessimism, he would choose the former because life is more agreeable to the optimist than it is to the pessimist. In James the moral idealism of Emerson and the democratic idealism of Whitman were fused about as well as they could be with the utilitarianism of the businessman and the materialism of the scientist. His mind, as Santayana has said, came nearer than any other to representing the American mind of his generation.

Thus James, being part mystic and part empiricist, tried to harmonize the antagonistic elements of idealism and materialism in the American character. His fellow pragmatist John Dewey, on the other hand, eschewed mysticism and built his philosophy on strictly material foundations. Accepting the Darwinian theory of evolution, he applied it also to the social process. Everything, according to Dewey, is changing from what was to what is, and from what is to what is to be, and nothing has value except as it has reference to this process. History is therefore of little account, and all present action is of uncertain value, because the grounds for determining its value do not yet completely exist. As one commentator has remarked, in Dewey's world there is always jam tomorrow, but never any jam today. Beyond question, this philosophy reflects the restless energy and opportunism of many, perhaps most, Americans of recent years. Whether, in the end, it will prove to be the friend or the enemy of idealism is still a debatable point.

The purpose of this essay, however, is not to present a digest of American philosophical thought, except as it may have influenced American literature. Usually the appearance of ideas in literature follows by a good many years their original pronouncement by philosophers and scientists. Moreover, American writers have sometimes been less ready to follow American philosophies than to embrace those of European origin. Hence we may expect to find in American literature of the late nineteenth century as much of Schopenhauer's pessimism as of Emerson's optimism. Early in the twentieth century the influence of the anti-democratic superman philosophy began to be felt, and later the psychoanalytical methods of Freud were adopted by critics as well as creative writers, sometimes with unfortunate results. None of these influences, however, were as overwhelming in their effect as the influence of scientific materialism, for in America "Science" has long been the infallible bible of our utilitarian religion of "Success."

The new era in American fiction began with the mild realism of William Dean Howells, a contemporary of Mark Twain, and reached its climax in the naturalism of Theodore Dreiser in the first quarter of the twentieth century, after which signs began to appear of a new era in the making. But before turning to Howells and the realistic movement in fiction, it is necessary to pause for a moment to consider another novelist whose work, though not in the fullest sense American, is too important to be overlooked. This was Henry James, younger brother of William, who placed the small section of American life that he knew under the microscope and described it with the minuteness and cold detachment of a bacteriologist. Most of his novels, and all his best works, were written before he became well acquainted with his brother's philosophical ideas. He was moral in his point of view, but his characters, the best of whom are women, such as Isabel Archer, the generous and true, and Madame Merle, the selfish and false, in *The Portrait of a Lady,* exist less in their own right as real human beings than as specimens for psychological analysis. Henry James is usually classified as a realist, though his realism was hardly more noticeable than Hawthorne's, and like Hawthorne's it was psychological rather than factual. Crudeness and immorality, however real, were extremely distasteful to him; on the other hand, he manifested little faith in average human nature and looked with distrust upon the turbulent democracy of his native country. His æsthetic idealism was too cold to warm the hearts of his countrymen.

Like Howells and Mark Twain, he migrated from West to East, but since he was born in New York he could not go east without leaving the country, which eventually he did, living mostly in London during his active literary career. In Mark Twain's stories much happens with little interpretation; in James's, little happens with much interpretation. If one is concerned mostly with surfaces, the other moves obscurely beneath the surface and his voice reaches us with confused reverberations. Since most of James's novels have to do with the problem of the American visiting or more permanently dwelling in Europe, they have a cosmopolitan air. This fact, together with the

difficulty of his style and his paucity of adventure, has
limited his audience in America to the few sophisticates
who find drawing room conversation as thrilling as hunting for buried treasure with Tom Sawyer.

Henry James was a man without a country, for he
could not interest himself in America and he was never
able to root his life solidly in England. The characters of
his novels appear and go like flotsam on the sea, unre-
lated to any permanent background. To use an Emersonian term, they lack polarity. So it seems to many a reader.
Perhaps the fault is rather that the reader hears no echo
of himself in James's voice or the voices of his characters,
but it comes to the same thing. James made his choice; he
wanted to write international novels. But there are no international novels, just as there are no international people. A man and his country are the two opposites of a
polarized life, and life does not really exist otherwise.
The persistent tendency to regionalism in the United
States is an evidence that a person writes best in and about
the region where his life is rooted and his heart feels at
home. A human being is not easily transplanted.

I should more readily criticize James for this aban-
donment of his country except that I recognize it as only
another manifestation of the characteristic American habit
of turning one's back upon what is in order to seek for
what might be, or ought to be, or is supposed to have been.
It is Thoreau's hound, and horse, and turtle dove that
forever lure the American away from the present into
the past or the future, the remote or the strange. The
pragmatists, as we have seen, have raised this longing to
live in the future into the dignity of a philosophy. James
thought he knew English life before he adopted it, but

after a while he discovered that he was more a stranger than he had at first seemed to be. Many Americans since James's time, believing that they had found their own country empty, left it for Europe; but it was they who were empty, not America, as they soon found. Some of them, like James, and perhaps misled by his example, stayed away too long and could be at home neither here nor there. Like Hawthorne's Wakefield they had lost their places in the procession of human life, or like Alley Oop in the comic strip they were islanded in time, only they had no time-machine to bring them back to their own era. But others who remained in America escaped into the past almost as effectually by borrowing the culture of the past. James had not discovered, with Emerson, that the soul "shall have society of its own rank" wherever it goes; if he had, American literature might have been the richer for his discovery.

William Dean Howells, the friend of Mark Twain and Henry James and the dedicated heir of James Russell Lowell, was peculiarly fortunate in his literary associations. A native of Ohio, born in 1837, he spent the Civil War years as consul in Venice, but returned to America in 1865 and settled in Boston. In his youth he had written for newspapers in Ohio, and it was easy for him to turn now to editorial work. He was editor of *The Atlantic Monthly* for many years, and afterwards, in New York, he filled an editorial chair in the offices of *Harper's Magazine*. He began writing novels only after many years of experience in other literary forms and after an extensive study of European models. Like James he was cosmopolitan in his tastes, but he preferred to live in America, and became closely identified with the movement towards realism in fiction, of which he remained the chief advocate and exemplar for three decades. He read the Russian Turgenev, the French Zola, and finally Tolstoy. In Turgenev he found excellent examples of the social studies that came to form so large a part of his work. Zola's naturalism cleared the way for Howells' own realism, which was much milder; it should be milder, he argued, because America had not felt the poverty and class conflicts that had torn the Old World, and therefore to be realistic it was not necessary to picture the violent and the ugly Tolstoy he read especially in the eighties, when there were symptoms of a new interest in social reform and even socialistic projects in the United States.

Howells' realism was a compromise between the method of romance and the method of naturalism as exemplified by Zola, and though it is theoretically sound it has never proved very effective. However, it may be that Howells did not give his method a fair trial, and the reason for his failure is to be found in his temperament. He shrank instinctively from the ugly and the painful, and he was too clear-eyed and clear-headed to harbor illusions of goodness and beauty. He cultivated the belief that in America there are no extremes, that people are neither very good nor very bad, and that the realistic novel must depict this mildly exciting life of average humanity. The chief objection to this interpretation of American life is that it is false. But if it were true it could not be made the basis of a deeply moving literature, which must have heroes and villains in more than average proportions and a conflict that is more than mildly exciting. Superficially his theory suggests Whitman, but Whitman had no such conception of the average man. His ringing challenge was,

"Produce great persons; the rest follows." This is as true in literature as it is in society.

Howells rarely produces great persons, but the greater the person, other things being equal, the greater the noval. To illustrate, let us compare two of his best known novels, *A Modern Instance* (1882) and *The Rise of Silas Lapham* (1885). The chief character in the former is Bartley Hubbard, an average man, a journalist, who allows his moral nature to disintegrate slowly under the steady pressure of circumstances until he passes from venial faults to the misappropriation of money, thence to wife desertion, and finally to violent death at the hand of a man whom he had publicly slandered. The story is well done and excellent in its kind, but it leaves the reader with a depressed feeling because there is nothing heroic in it. The chief character of *The Rise of Silas Lapham* is like Matthias in Edwin Arlington Robinson's poem *Matthias at the Door:* he must fail in the world of material values before he can succeed in the world of spiritual values. Silas Lapham makes a fortune and then loses it, but in losing his money he preserves his moral integrity.

Howells was a steadying force in literature, but it was futile for him to attempt to halt the movement away from romanticism while standing on the middle ground that he chose to call realism. In the end he was a bridge instead of a barrier between Hawthorne and Dreiser. He was idealistic in his aims, but his methods rendered those aims ineffectual.

The influence of James is to be seen at its best in the novels of Edith Wharton, whose family and friends belonged to the class of wealthy cosmopolitans whose entire energies were concentrated upon what has been called "the art of living" to distinguish it from the kind of living in which regular employment is an important consideration. In many ways, particularly in the clarity of her style, her work is an improvement over that of James. Although most of her best novels were written while she was resident in France, the experience on which they were based belongs to her American years, and the characters she created are geographically and culturally centered in America. The import of her social criticism is indicated in the titles of her characteristic books: *The House of Mirth* (1905), *The Custom of the Country* (1913), *The Age of Innocence* (1920). These and other novels deal with the problems arising within a highly conventionalized social group as it begins to disintegrate under the impact of radical ideas. Like James she suffers the disadvantage of writing for people with aristocratic tastes in a democratic country, and it is probable that she has accomplished about as much as can possibly be done under these circumstances.

The influence of Howells has been more extensive but less definite than that of James. Most of those who looked to him for encouragement in their battle for realism against romanticism were more radical than he and moved further in the direction of naturalism as represented in the novels of Zola. They also went further than Howells in adopting the methods of journalism and propaganda in place of the orthodox methods of literary criticism.

The most prominent of these new realists was Hamlin Garland, a Middle Westerner, farm-born and self-educated, who set the fashion for fiction in the new style with a series of grim stories depicting the unremitting toil, hardship, and bitterness in the lives of the farmers of the

Dakotas, later published in two volumes, *Main-Trav-elled Roads* (1891) and *Prairie Folks* (1893). These stories were based upon his personal experience and ob-servation, but he also had an ulterior motive of social re-form; for he had become a convert to the anti-monopoly economics of Henry George, who affirmed that a man has the right to the use of as much of the country's natural wealth as may be necessary to supply the ordinary wants of life, so long as he may use it without interfering with the equal rights of any other person. In a sense Garland was not a literary man by natural inclination though he was by profession; his greatest enthusiasms were humani-tarian, and the best of his early years were devoted to the ideal of righting wrongs and building a more equitable social order. Later his ardor cooled, and his last years were occupied in recalling the days of his youth, which, now that they were thirty years agone, seemed far better than they did to the youth who wrote *Main-Travelled Roads*.

Two years after the publication of *Main-Travelled Roads*, Stephen Crane, a young newspaper reporter barely old enough to vote, wrote a little novel entitled *Maggie: A Girl of the Streets* which, since no publisher would take it, he printed at his own cost. Maggie was hounded out of her home by a brutal mother, and having passed through the successive stages of factory girl, kept mistress, and prostitute, found life unendurable and drowned herself. The critics objected to the story because it was left stark and ugly, unaccompanied by sentiment or moral precept, although the moral implications would have been clear enough to a generation less blinded than Crane's by self-righteousness and sentimentality. With the encouragement of Garland and Howells, Crane wrote *The Red Badge of Courage,* a realistic description of the feelings of a common soldier in a battle of the Civil War, which proved so popular that the publishers agreed to issue his story of Maggie.

Although Crane's realism is more vivid than that of his older contemporaries, it is still illuminated by a sense of the dignity of man and the superiority of moral values over material values. The soldier in *The Red Badge of Courage* is ashamed when he runs from physical danger and proud when he faces it. In one of Crane's later short stories, "The Open Boat," he would have us believe that, though nature is not a beneficent helper in the human struggle, neither is she treacherous; and that, though in human experience virtue is not always rewarded, it is appreciated and admired. Crane's death at twenty-nine was a genuine loss to American literature.

Another talented young novelist of this period who died before his talents matured was Frank Norris, born in 1870 in Chicago and educated there and at the University of California and Harvard. Impatient with the fad of local color hunting, he planned his work on an epic scale and was ambitious to paint the whole of America on one great canvas. His plan was to write an epic of wheat, in three parts. He completed only two. The first is *The Octopus* (1901), which describes the growing of the wheat on the great ranches of California, and the bitter conflict between the ranchers and the railroad corporation, which is the octopus. The second is *The Pit* (1903), which describes the distribution of the wheat and the struggle of speculators on the Chicago Board of Trade to control it. The third was to be called *The Wolf,* and it was to deal with the consumption of the wheat and picture the role that America plays in feeding the millions of Europe. If he could have completed this plan as he conceived it, he would have accomplished a work unique in American literature; as it stands it is not only incomplete, but even in the parts completed it lacks the sublimity and unity that so great a theme requires. *The Octopus*, though more diffuse than *The Pit*, has poetic passages that suggest the cosmic sweep of Whitman and the emotional intensity of Melville. Before undertaking his trilogy of wheat, Norris wrote a naturalistic novel, *McTeague*, after the model of Zola; but I do not think he was genuinely in sympathy with either the method or the philosophy of naturalism. On the contrary, he was definitely idealistic in his outlook and inclined to romanticism in his method. If he had lived ten or twenty years longer (he died in 1902), he might have corrected his weaknesses and produced a really great work.

The work of Norris and Crane has not been popular, whereas that of Jack London, whose name is usually linked with theirs, made the author a small fortune. London was born in California in 1876, and made that state his home until his death, which occurred in 1916. His childhood and youth were full of poverty, vagabondage, and hard labor, but he seems to have enjoyed the struggle. He had tremendous vitality and devoured books as voraciously as he ate and drank, but his knowledge was superficial and narrow. He was by profession a scientific materialist, basing his philosophy upon what he had read of Darwin, Huxley, and Spencer, and he had some knowledge of the German philosopher Nietzsche. The idea which seems to have dominated his life was the Darwin-

ian conception of the struggle for survival. His own struggle and his remarkable ability to overcome every obstacle
confirmed his belief in this idea. He was also interested in
Marxian economics, and during the last ten or twelve
years of his life was closely identified with socialist propaganda in America. Here were three ways of interpreting
human life that were somewhat inharmonious: his materialistic interpretation of evolution, his romantic concept of the superman, after Nietzsche, and his championship of the common man through the dogma of the class
struggle. His personal experience in the school of hard
knocks taught him that the strongest man always wins,
and his scientific reading led him to believe in a purely
materialistic universe; hence it appeared that he was justified by the laws of nature in getting what he wanted if
he could. His phenomenal success no doubt suggested to
him that he might be a superman, and if he was a superman he could afford to be magnanimous and extend a
helping hand to the toiling masses. This interpretation of
his motives may do him an injustice, for he was capable of
an impulsive generosity without thought of self.

His best book is *The Call of the Wild* (1903), a con-
cise and gripping story of a dog in Alaska who feels an
atavistic "call" from his ancient wolf forbears which im-
pels him eventually to abandon the haunts of men and
join his contemporary wolf cousins. This general theme
is intensely romantic and is closely akin to less scientific
romances like the "Tarzan of the Apes" series. London
wrote several books about prehistoric man, the best known
of which is entitled *Before Adam* (1907). But the theme
of atavism is not perhaps the most characteristic element
in *The Call of the Wild*. In the dog's experience between

the time he was stolen away from his easy life as a pampered pet and the day of his final return to savagery, he had many a life-and-death fight and many a narrow escape. He always won because he was bigger and smarter or luckier than his enemy. Several times he almost lost because he was too much like the civilized human friends with whom he had lived as a pup, and the author persuades the reader to admire him more as he reverts to the ways of his savage ancestors.

One should not too hastily conclude that the law of the jungle is the law which Jack London recommended to govern human conduct, although it must be admitted that he rated it quite high. Wolf Larsen, the wolfish hero of his second most popular book, *The Sea Wolf* (1904), is as despicable and horrible as the wolfish dog of *The Call of the Wild* is admirable, and the reason is that whereas the dog kills from physical need, the man kills from meanness and spiritual depravity. But doubtless London had a vague purpose in mind of making Wolf Larsen an object lesson, because he is finally stricken with paralysis and loses the struggle with his rival, whose weapons are human rather than brutish. Moreover, in the autobiographical novel *Martin Eden* (1909), the hero, a writer, wins fame and riches only to discover that his life has no further usefulness, and so, self-defeated at the age of thirty, he commits suicide. It would probably be incorrect to say, therefore, that Jack London was devoid of moral idealism, but one is compelled to believe that, so far as he has made his views known in his books, it was subordinated to a materialistic philosophy of force.

The last of the naturalists to be discussed in this chapter, Theodore Dreiser, was born in 1871, educated in Indiana, and trained as a newspaper reporter in Chicago, St. Louis, and other cities. After his reporting days he turned to magazine editing and the writing of fiction, and for forty years now he has been a legendary figure in American literature. His first novel, *Sister Carrie*, was published as early as 1900, but had no success, and Dreiser produced no other until *Jennie Gerhardt*, in 1911. He followed this with *The Financier* in 1912, *The Titan* in 1914, and *The "Genius"* in 1915, after which he wrote no important fiction until he brought out *An American Tragedy* in 1925. This last novel, a two volume work which promises to be acknowledged as his masterpiece, has been followed by no other major fiction.

Sister Carrie was an ambitious and rather unscrupulous girl who became a successful actress. On her way to fame she lived with first one man and then another; she went blithely forward, but one of the men, who had left a wife and children for her, is made to suffer progressive moral decay until he is carried at last to a pauper's grave. Jennie Gerhardt was much like Carrie, only more expertly portrayed, and certainly more pliant. Then Dreiser gave us his heroes. The Financier and the Titan were portraits of business tycoons drawn after the model of a real American financier. This hero's methods of accomplishing his desires are very much like the methods of London's superman heroes, except that Dreiser's men incline to assert their manhood in orgies of sex rather than orgies of bloody battle. Change the scenery and transfer the financier into the softer world of art and you have his next hero, the Genius. In *An American Tragedy* the principal character, Clyde Griffiths, is far from heroic. On the contrary, he is a moral weakling and in all other respects mediocre. He is somewhat like Bartley Hubbard, the weak hero of Howells' *A Modern Instance*, without Bartley's rudimentary conscience. He is living with a factory girl, who is about to bear him a child, but he wants to improve his worldly position by marrying another girl, and he cannot think of anything better to do than to drown the one he does not want. In all of these novels characters act to fulfill their desires without regard to moral principles, sometimes succeeding and winning happiness and sometimes failing and suffering unhappiness and pain. The author is apparently indifferent; he reports what he knows and has no opinion on the meaning of his facts. This is obviously the method of the newspaper reporter. It is not the method of the scientist, because the scientist is intensely interested in meanings; in fact he collects facts for no purpose but to examine them for meanings.

Carl Van Doren calls Dreiser a "cosmic philosopher" to whom man is so small a figure that the difference between the heroic and the unheroic is not noticed. But he tells us that this cosmic philosopher cannot understand the cosmos which he beholds, and is in this respect worse off than the pygmy men themselves, for they can at least find temporary or partial support on relative values. This is the fallacy of much recent thinking by people who conclude that because man's standards of good and evil have no meaning in the cosmic processes they can have none in human relationships. Emerson was also a cosmic philosopher, but he insisted that there is a law for man that is not applicable to physical nature, namely the moral law. In relieving human beings of all necessity except the satisfaction of animal desires, Dreiser appears, like Jack London, to hold a purely materialistic view of the human world. To these Americans, man is an animal motivated like other animals by desires and fears that arise from obscure chemical arrangements over which he exercises no authority.

Although Dreiser is unable to form a judgment on human conduct, he is moved to pity those who are made to suffer from maladjustments. This pity must spring either from a sense of injustice, which implies value judgments, or from a bland regret that cosmic laws cannot be violated with impunity to gratify the whim of every creature of desire, no matter how insignificant or selfish. In the one case he disavows the philosophy of all his novels, and in the other he betrays an extraordinary lack of rational consistency. It is incredible that Dreiser, serious and deliberate as he was, could have labored forty years to picture in its minutest details a world which he believed did not exist; I conclude, therefore, that he was a thorough and sincere materialist, and that he saw nothing more in the moral code at any given place and time than a contrivance of a class or majority group to compel the individual to conform to the conventions established by the group. Weak individuals yield readily to the group pattern, but strong individuals—that is, individuals powerfully driven by desire—rebel against this compulsion and tend to conduct themselves as they wish, independent of any moral code. If the individual is sufficiently strong he can usually defy the moral code; at least that has been the case in America in the past century. The people whose lives become tragic are those mediocre or erratic individuals in whom desire is strong enough to drive them into immoral acts but not strong enough to overcome or modify the force of public opinion. The hero of *An American Tragedy* is such a tragic individual. Dreiser does not blame the individual for his power, or the use of it, to gratify his desires in defiance of the social code; on the contrary he admires him as a superior individual. Neither does he blame the weak individual for his weakness, but he pities him if he suffers at the hands of the dominant group, and in this pity there is an implied criticism of the group for the exercise of its power. It seems therefore, as I said before, that Dreiser's philosophy, in so far as it is correctly represented in his novels, is individualistic and antisocial, a kind of laissez-faire principle operating in the moral sphere.

In the materialism of Theodore Dreiser, American thought as expressed in literature reached the final point in that decline from idealism some of the main features of which I have pointed out in this chapter and in the one preceding. The idealism of Emerson and the materialism of Dreiser are the opposite poles of American philosophy. Many factors combined to produce this change, the most powerful being the advance of science. Science made the machine, which enslaves the body of man by eliminating physical strength as a power in human affairs; and science produced the philosophy of scientific determinism, which enslaves the mind of man by rendering impotent the individual will. The new philosophy is like Calvinism in denying to man any power or dignity, but it differs in this, that whereas Calvinism postulates a universe directed by a rational Being who is sometimes moved to pity and protect the individual, scientific determinism postulates a universe without rational direction but driven blindly by impersonal laws that are totally alien to the reason and the moral idealism of the human mind. Believing in such a world, the individual is persuaded to abandon both reason and morality and fall back upon his animal appetites and instincts for guidance. I do not accuse Mr. Dreiser of advocating reversion from civilization to savagery, for it is well known that he is a most humane person; nevertheless, the tendency of his philosophy as represented in his fiction is to lead man in that direction, because it deprives him of faith in the possibility of creating a moral universe which will free him from his slavery to the physical universe.

VIII

Contemporary Fiction

While the influence of Theodore Dreiser on contemporary American fiction has been great, his successors have been more inclined to imitate his naturalistic methods than to embrace his deterministic philosophy. Americans have an almost insatiable appetite for sentiment and sensation, either or both at once, but they are quickly surfeited with fatalism. They sometimes debauch themselves with fatalism as they do with alcohol, but the more they are debauched, the more they become sentimental. Of Dreiser's successors, there will be more to say later in this chapter; of his contemporaries, many are rapidly being forgotten, although in their day their sentimentality was more popular than his naturalism. Where he had his thousands of readers, Harold Bell Wright and Zane Grey had their millions. But there were other popular writers more deserving of esteem than the two just named. Booth Tarkington, with his Penrod stories and his novels of manners, the best of which was *Alice Adams*, carried on the traditions of Mark Twain and William Dean Howells. Winston Churchill's historical novels and novels of social problems, although lacking in great literary distinction, dealt honestly and intelligently with the ideals and aspirations of the American people.

Somewhat younger than Dreiser were Willa Cather and Sinclair Lewis, of whom I shall speak in more detail presently, and perhaps half a dozen others of significance. Ellen Glasgow wrote many novels of character and social criticism, the best of which is *Barren Ground*, which appeared in the same year with *An American Tragedy*. This is the story of a woman who valued an ideal more than happiness and won a moral victory from what appeared to be defeat. Sherwood Anderson, like Dreiser a rebel against things as they are, was less a naturalist than a frustrated idealist turned primitive who attributed to the objective world the vague restlessness and dislocation that existed within himself. James Branch Cabell agreed with the naturalists that ours is a poor sort of world, but it moved him to laughter rather than disgust; yet he would not permit himself the bad taste to laugh at the real world, and so, half in earnest and half in satanic mischief, he created for himself a realm of high romance, to which he addressed his ironic laughter. Joseph Hergesheimer also created a hollow world of shining surfaces, but he intended no jest, for many a reader, and perhaps even the author himself, took it to be real. Edna Ferber was one of several who exploited the achievements of American pioneers for stirring fiction and motion pictures. Few of these have lasting value; but there is one book that surpasses all others of this kind, although our right to claim it for American literature might be questioned, since it was written in Norwegian by a man who did not come to America until his twentieth year. I refer to Ole Rölvaag's *Giants in the Earth*, the epic story of Norwegian pioneers on the windswept plains of South Dakota. Its style is grimly realistic, but the power that sustains these humble men in their struggle with inclement nature was of the spirit as well as of the body. For a wholly satisfying treatment of pioneer life in American fiction, however, we must turn to the novels of Willa Cather.

Born in Virginia in 1876, Willa Cather removed with her parents to Nebraska when she was nine years old. Here she became intimate with the Bohemians, Scandinavians, Germans, and other foreign-born pioneers who were neighbors of her family. Graduating from the University of Nebraska, she went to Pittsburgh, where she did newspaper work and taught English in the high school for several years. Between 1906 and 1911 she was a member of the editorial staff of *McClure's Magazine*. It was during this time that she became acquainted with the New England realist, Sarah Orne Jewett, who became her friend and adviser. While a student in the University she had read the novels of Henry James and admired them. Like Edith Wharton, she belongs to the school of James, although she betrays the fact only in the feeling for style which she has in common with him.

I shall comment upon only five of Miss Cather's books. Two of these, *O Pioneers!* (1913) and *My Antonia* (1918), are based upon recollections of her childhood in Nebraska. Two others, *Death Comes for the Archbishop* (1927) and *Shadows on the Rock* (1931), are studies of transplanted Catholic cultures in American frontier regions, the one in New Mexico about the middle of the nineteenth century and the other in Quebec early in the eighteenth. The last of the five, the recently published *Sapphira and the Slave Girl*, has its setting in upland Virginia in the decade preceding the Civil War.

Willa Cather is at her best in delineating the charac-

ters of women, and in her two pioneer novels of Nebraska
she has created two of the strongest and most glowing
women in American fiction. Alexandra Bergson, the hero-
ine of *O Pioneers!*, is a Swedish-American girl who, after
her father's death, holds her family to the land and saves
it, at the same time growing by her efforts into a character
as wholesome and almost as solid as the land itself. In *My
Antonia*, which many readers believe to be her best book,
she has created in Antonia Shimerda, the daughter of a
Bohemian immigrant, a woman of a rich and strong nature, whose instinct for motherhood and whose influence
for good in the family and in the community make her
one of the truly great heroines of literature. Unlike Alexandra Bergson, Antonia does not remain on the land; as
a girl she goes, like many others from the farm families,
into the nearby town to do housework. There she falls in
with a group of girls who lack her rich but simple nature
and presently becomes attached to a worthless man, who
abandons her and leaves her with an illegitimate child.
But though Antonia loses her respectability, she remains
good and strong, and eventually she returns to the country, marries a worthy farmer, and becomes the mother of
a large family. This family is her triumph, for she has a
genius for motherhood. Although Willa Cather does not
say so, Antonia is precisely the type of woman that Whitman celebrates in *Leaves of Grass* as the ideal mother of
men. Her dominant quality was love, whereas the dominant quality of Alexandra Bergson was will; the two together exemplify all that is needed by the pioneer woman.
These women were not figments of the author's imagination, but characters such as she had known in Nebraska,
and they stand as a guarantee that goodness, and strength,

and faithful love, and the power to face disappointment and disaster without losing faith are qualities which this generation possesses as the heritage of its pioneer mothers. It is comforting to turn from the frivolity and cynicism of so much recent literature to these strong, wholesome, immortal women.

The atmosphere of *Death Comes for the Archbishop* is quite different. The land is there still, but not the fertile fields and dreaming pasture lands of eastern Nebraska. It is the desert sands, cool and mysterious in the moonlight, and the barren mountains, turquoise and silver against the late afternoon sun. The tone and style of the novel is in keeping with the sensuous yet delicate and spiritualized beauty of the landscape in the half-lights of dawn and twilight. Although there is a minimum of plot, there is plenty of action, some of it violent and bloody. The main characters are Bishop Jean Latour and his vicar, Father Joseph Vaillant, two Catholic priests whose heroic courage in this lawless wilderness is but a part of their daily task. The famous Indian scout, Kit Carson, comes into the story, and the Bishop is pleased with him at first sight. "As he stood there in his buckskin clothes one felt in him standards, loyalties, a code which is not easily put into words, but which is instantly felt when two men who live by it come together by chance." Here is the core of Willa Cather's idealism—that men should have standards, loyalties, a code to live by. Kit Carson was wholly illiterate and had no formal religious training. He was a product of the frontier, and his life had been too full of action to allow much time for thought or meditation; yet, as Willa Cather says of him, "he had preserved a clean sense of honour and a compassionate heart."

Similar in style and treatment, *Shadows on the Rock* is even more silvery in tone and color. It is a story of old Quebec two hundred years ago, and though noblemen, adventurers, and men of passion move in and out, the center of interest is always in the life of the little girl, Cecile Auclair. One feels that amidst all the restless movement, something in human life should and does remain fixed and unchanging. The outer symbol of this unchanging element in life may be the Catholic Church, but the real thing is the abiding sense of moral power in the character of the individual human being.

Willa Cather's latest novel, *Sapphira and the Slave Girl,* does not have the beauty of *Shadows on the Rock* and *Death Comes for the Archbishop* nor the fine character studies *O Pioneers!* and *My Antonia,* but it is written with the directness and sincerity that are characteristic of the author's entire work. This book needed to be written in order to fill out the pattern of American life in her fiction. She had written of pioneers, of immigrants in the West, of the Catholic Southwest and Canada, of artists both in the West and in New York, but until now she had written nothing about Virginia, the place of her birth. As usual, she has chosen her setting at a place and time where life has something of the pioneer quality but is not far removed from older communities in which settled conditions prevail. This setting gives her a chance to throw the old and the new into vivid contrast, and it also favors greater variety and richness in the characters.

The story involves four principal characters: Sapphira, a woman past middle age and confined to an invalid's wheel chair, her husband, Henry Colbert, her widowed daughter, Rachel, and her pretty mulatto slave girl, Nancy, of whom she is jealous. There is more to the novel, of course, than the foolish jealousy of a proud woman who resents her approaching old age and her physical helplessness, but that is the key to the plot. The character of Rachel Blake is not unlike that of Antonia, and Henry Colbert, the miller, is a man of moral strength and humane ideals. One cannot escape the feeling that the author intends Henry and his daughter Rachel to represent a more admirable type of American character than the plantation aristocracy from which Sapphira came or the crude and insensitive rustics who live among the Virginia hills. Life grows stale and suspicious in long established cultures, whereas the new and restless life of the frontier is crude and ugly. Somewhere between these two extremes there is a life that is stable yet evolving on sure foundations, and this is life at its best. Like Emerson and Whitman, Miss Cather believes that the strength of the nation is in the character of the individuals who compose it. Somewhere she has said, "The history of every country begins in the heart of a man or a woman." With few exceptions, her characters are morally strong and sure of their strength.

Sinclair Lewis, like Willa Cather, grew up in the Middle West, but his native state, Minnesota, had passed the frontier stage before his time. The town of Sauk Center, where he was reared, was typical of thousands of small towns throughout agricultural America; it was neither heroic nor picturesque, only commonplace and dull. Or so it seemed to the sensitive and perhaps romantic boy who became the most sensational literary success of the present century. After attending Yale University, knocking about the country as a newspaper reporter, and working for a time as a publisher's reader, he wrote five nondescript apprentice novels and then, in 1920, electrified the reading public by producing his first great success, *Main Street*. Since that time he has written ten other novels, and in 1930 he received the Nobel Prize in literature, the first American to be so honored. His best novels, in the opinion of competent critics, are *Main Street*, *Babbitt* (1922), *Arrowsmith* (1925), and *Dodsworth* (1929). To these four novels some readers would wish to add a fifth, *Ann Vickers* (1933), but the rest of his work, all agree, is definitely inferior.

Main Street is a realistic picture, somewhat exaggerated, of the ugliness of the American small town and the stultifying dullness of the lives of the people who inhabit it. The book speaks for all those who have suffered from the narrow mindedness, the spiritual lethargy, and the self-satisfied ignorance so often engendered by such a life. At times Lewis is rather bitter, as if he had suffered from these things himself. But in reading his stories one never feels that the meanness of village life is the consequence of an inherent meanness of the human spirit; on the contrary, he always includes one character or more through whom he affirms his faith in the power of mind and character to overcome the prevailing meanness, or at least to refuse to yield to it. In *Main Street* Carol Kennicott is the valiant one. She has many faults, but she also has the courage to acknowledge defeat without bitterness or loss of faith. After running away from Gopher Prairie and staying two years, she returns to it and to her husband, but her spirit is unbroken. At the end she says: "But I have won in this: I've never excused my failures by sneering at my aspirations, by pretending to have gone beyond them. I do not admit that Main Street is as beautiful as it should be! I do not admit that Gopher Prairie is greater or more generous than Europe! I do not admit that dish-washing is enough to satisfy all women! I may not have fought the good fight, but I have kept the faith."

In Lewis's next novel, *Babbitt,* the city of Zenith is a magnified Gopher Prairie, and the vices of one are the vices of the other. Babbitt has stirrings of idealism, but he is easy-going and yields to the currents of business and social practice. He gives up his plan to be a lawyer when he falls in love and turns to real estate for quick returns. He winks at the dishonesty of his firm because not to wink at it would bring him into unpleasant controversy with his associates in business. He is unfaithful to his wife be-cause he is bored, and then is ashamed of himself. It was easy and profitable to adjust himself to the materialistic and unimaginative mode of life which the city had made standard. But it is perhaps to Babbitt's credit that he could not yield wholly. He had just enough light to make his darkness visible. He was therefore, like Carol Kennicott, a failure. It is too late for him to remake his own life, but he derives some satisfaction in the hope that his son will do better. "Don't be scared of the family," he admonishes his son. "No, nor of all Zenith. Nor of yourself, the way I've been."

The most important of Lewis's novels from the point of view of this study, and perhaps the most important from any point of view, is the one that followed *Babbitt, Arrowsmith.* In this novel the emphasis is upon the ideal-ism of the main character, who is a physician and a scien-tist. Just as *Babbitt* reveals the cant and chicanery of business, so *Arrowsmith* reveals the cant and chicanery of the medical profession and even of scientific institutions. But unlike Babbitt, Arrowsmith has the strength to break away from the materialistic influences and pursue his ideal. It is not an easy victory and comes only after many defeats and compromises. It is his desire to search out truth for its own sake, not for some ulterior end, even though the end be worthy. With this desire lesser desires conflict. First it is love, and later material success and worldly fame. In the end he sacrifices love, wealth, and fame for a life of obscurity and hardship in the laboratory which he and a fellow-bacteriologist have improvised in the woods of Vermont. "I feel as if I were beginning to work now," Arrowsmith says to his friend in the last paragraph of the novel. "This new quinine stuff may prove pretty good. We'll plug along on it for two or three years, and maybe we'll get something permanent—and probably we'll fail." The author leaves us with the conviction that failure and success are words of no meaning unless they refer to work that has value in and for itself, independent of worldly standards.

Dodsworth is a novel representing the career of a rich automobile manufacturer in Zenith who retires from business, travels in Europe with his worldly wife and is finally estranged from her, and then returns to America with the hope of doing something really creative. The important fact about Dodsworth is that he does want something more from life than the making and spending of money; he has an inner need that is the measure of his spiritual power. Several of Lewis's characters have this impulse to idealism, although it is not often noticed by the critics amidst the more obvious satire on American bigotry and crudeness. Probe the depths of Lewis's best characters and you find something very much like Emerson's self-reliance.

Willa Cather and Sinclair Lewis represent the generation that came to maturity before the first World War and were not fundamentally affected by it. The two writers next to be discussed, John Dos Passos, born in 1896, and Ernest Hemingway, born in 1898, were both active participants in the war, were both volunteers in foreign service rather than in the American service, and both lived much in Europe. They speak for the war generation, and their work reflects the disillusionment suffered by millions of young men throughout the world who were soldiers in that war. These young men were allowed and even encouraged during the war to live as if the value of life were in the experience of the senses. It was a way to forget danger and endure hardships. But when the war was over many of them went on living as if they were still soldiers trying not to think of tomorrow's battle and the muck of the trenches. The psychology that was useful in war became a demoralizing force in peace, and it was the more unfortunate because it infected many who had not been in the war and many adolescents whose moral balance was seriously upset.

John Dos Passos is described by a recent critic as a sensitive idealist who writes as he does because he has been offended and disillusioned by the unidealistic world that made the war. I have no reason to question the accuracy of this description; but, granting its truth, the idealism of Mr. Dos Passos is of no consequence to literary history unless it appears in his contributions to literature. So far, I have been unable to discover much evidence of it there. His sensitiveness may have a negative expression; that is, he may exaggerate the ugliness of life because the ugliness has hurt him. As a matter of fact, his characters do not act as if they hate what they do; on the contrary, most of them act as if they like it. It is doubtful, therefore, whether Dos Passos serves the cause of beauty by representing life as ugly.

The most important work done by Dos Passos to date is the trilogy he calls *U.S.A.* It consists of three separate novels, originally published as *The 42nd Parallel* (1930), *Nineteen-Nineteen* (1932), and *The Big Money* (1936). The style is experimental and suggestive at once of James Joyce, Virginia Woolf, T. S. Eliot's poetry, and the morning newspaper. The materials of the novel consist of four kinds: a narrative of fictional events, a series of newspaper headlines and paragraphs parallel in time and mood with the imagined events, a series of biographical sketches of famous men of our time, and a consecutive narrative called "The Camera Eye" which appears to be autobiographical. This complex arrangement, which is probably a device intended to assist the reader in comprehending the whole of American life as related to the lives of the story characters, becomes rather confusing and even depressing in the course of the nearly fifteen hundred pages of the three novels. I shall not attempt to summarize these stories, for there are a dozen individual narratives interwoven. There is a great deal of swearing and drinking and promiscuous sex relations. In general the characters fall into three classes: the ruthless and powerful who get what they want, the stolid and laborious who help them and seem content in vassalage, and the purposeless drifters who ask nothing more of life than the privilege of getting drunk and making love and talking about how vile life is. The author doubtless has a different conception of how life ought to be or might be, but he does not so inform his readers.

Yet Dos Passos probably has a purpose beyond mere entertainment. The very magnitude of the work and the deliberate complexity of the structure indicate that he did not undertake it lightly. There is an echo of Sandburg, and perhaps also of Whitman, in the preface to the trilogy in which he undertakes to tell his readers what the U.S.A. is and stands for. But there is nothing in this preface, and very little in the book, to suggest Whitman's or Sandburg's faith. Here is the body of America, but where is the soul? Sometimes in "The Camera Eye" the author hints that he may be aiming at something better than mere reporting, as in the following passage: ". . . while I go home after a drink and a hot meal and read (with some difficulty in the Loeb Library trot) the epigrams of Martial and ponder the course of history and what leverage might pry the owners loose from power and bring back (I too Walt Whitman) our storybook democracy." It would be pleasant to think that this is an endorsement of Whitman's philosophy, but the adjective "storybook" is hardly the one for an author to use to describe something he really believes in.

Ernest Hemingway, like Dos Passos a product of the war, has a formula for his novels. The hero is going to die (no matter how) in a few hours or a few days or a few months, but before he dies he compresses the whole of a lifetime of experience into the interval. Of course he does not always die, but his action is motivated by the thought that he will. This experience, needless to say, is one in which sexual love predominates. Whereas Dos Passos sees life as a complex pattern of many people and events, Hemingway sees it as concentrated emotion and decisive action involving few persons. His stories are more intense than comprehensive. For this reason, perhaps, he is particularly effective in the short story.

Hemingway has written a number of novels, but the only one that has any value for the history of idealism is his latest and undoubtedly his best work so far, *For Whom the Bell Tolls*. The theme of the story is suggested by the following excerpt from the prose writings of John Donne, which the author quotes as a kind of motto, and from which he draws his title:

No man is an Iland, intire of it selfe; every man is a peece of the Continent, a part of the maine; if a Clod bee washed away by the Sea, Europe is the lesse, as well as if a Promontorie were, as well as if a Mannor of thy friends or of thine owne were; any mans death diminishes me, because I am involved in Mankinde; And therefore never send to know for whom the bell tolls; It tolls for thee.

The hero of the story is Robert Jordan, an instructor in Spanish in an American university, who, being in Spain at the outbreak of the revolution, enlists in the loyalist army. Because he knows something of the use of dynamite in blasting, he is charged with the duty of blowing up a bridge over which the fascist troops are expected to pass within four days. He blows up the bridge successfully, but in his attempt to escape his horse is shot and falls on him. He cannot escape because his leg is broken; the rest of his party ride off and leave him there alone to sell his life as dearly as possible. As he lies there waiting for death he is content, for he believes that in losing his own life he has helped the cause of others fighting for freedom and a better world.

As I interpret the book, Hemingway means that the cause of the Spanish loyalists is the cause of freedom everywhere, and that what they gain or lose is gained or lost by the whole world. Although Jordan is a foreigner in Spain and is not a communist, he realizes that the loyalists are not fighting for themselves alone, but for him and for all men who love liberty. He therefore thinks it his duty to fight with them. No man, as Donne said, can live to himself, as an island; still less can a nation draw away from the rest of the world and make its own life selfishly and independently.

It is not disgust with life that makes Robert Jordan content to die. On the contrary, life has become especially desirable because only three days before he has met a Spanish girl living among the mountain people and has fallen deeply in love with her. The love story, although important, is nevertheless subordinated to the development of the theme of duty. In this, *For Whom the Bell Tolls* is strikingly different from Hemingway's earlier novels. Jordan is content to die precisely because life is good and the world good. There with his broken leg, struggling to hold on to consciousness and fighting the impulse to take his own life, he thinks to himself: "I have fought for what I believed in for a year now. If we win here we will win everywhere. The world is a fine place and worth the fighting for and I hate very much to leave it." And thinking of the loyalist battle that he hopes he has helped to win, he continues: "I want everything and I will take whatever I get. If this attack is no good another one will be." Thus in the very hour of his death he is thankful for the life he has had and is confident that in the end his cause will win.

It is not merely in Robert Jordan's dying reflections that we find the ideals of faith, courage, and hope. The entire action of the book tends to emphasize these ideals. There is little or no evidence here of the cynicism and disillusionment that were seen in Hemingway's early work. Even the bandits who helped the hero to destroy the bridge are not altogether bad. Indeed, one of the most heartening aspects of the book is the unexpected intelligence, courage, and honor displayed by these picturesque mountain people, though brutalized by war and forced to live in caves like animals. Altogether, *For Whom the Bell Tolls* is a powerful testimonial to the survival of idealism in American literature today, even in the work of a hard-boiled realist.

John Dos Passos and Ernest Hemingway are still in their early middle age, and the latter at least appears to have moved away from the mood of disillusionment and pessimism towards a more hopeful and optimistic mood. But it is not likely that they can ever wholly escape from the effects of their war years. The half-dozen novelists yet to be discussed in this chapter, mostly younger men, were not directly concerned in the war, although they were old enough to have been seriously affected by the spiritual letdown afterwards.

Three of these, William Faulkner of Mississippi, Erskine Caldwell of Georgia, and James T. Farrell of Chicago, belong to the school of naturalism in fiction. Faulkner seems obsessed with the horror and cruelty of human life, and under different circumstances might have been a romancer in the manner of Poe. He pictures the decadence and degradation of certain isolated families in the old South, the members of which are often afflicted with idiocy, sexual perversion, and criminal tendencies. Caldwell informs us, though with a touch of relieving humor, of the poverty and spiritual starvation, with their consequent misery and crime, of the class of Georgia share-croppers represented in the well-known novel and play, *Tobacco Road*. Farrell writes of the lower middle class Irish of Chicago. Like Caldwell, although more objective, he seems to have social aims in his writing and may be said to seek to accomplish the improvement of American life by dwelling upon its sordid aspects. It is generally agreed that Farrell's best work so far is the trilogy *Studs Lonigan*. Some critics blame the brutality and spiritual poverty of Studs Lonigan on society, but I cannot agree with them. At any rate I cannot see what society can do to prevent an occasional Studs Lonigan among many others who are quite unlike him. He is simply a "tough guy" whose counterpart has existed in all times and places and probably will continue so to exist. His is a personal, not a social, problem, and so far as I can judge, his end was neither tragic nor worse than might reasonably be expected. He was a moral weakling for whose protection I fear no social "system" can ever be devised; his occasional repentance and vague stirrings of aspiration are merely part of the veil of sentimentality by which such people hide their own meanness from themselves. In all three of these writers, but especially in Farrell, we can trace the influence of Theodore Dreiser.

Like the three novelists just discussed, John P. Marquand is concerned with morally decadent people. He is not a naturalist, however, but what, for lack of a more accurate term, one might call a romantic realist. He writes of New England gentility of the last two generations, and contrasts its weakness and superficiality with the strength and effectiveness of the middle nineteenth century New England gentility. He treats his characters with a cynical indulgence which does not totally hide his own faith, though weak, in the power of the old New England idealism to come to life again. His best known novels are *The Late George Apley* (1936), *Wickford Point* (1939), and *H. H. Pulham Esquire* (1941).

I have reserved the novels of Thomas Wolfe and John Steinbeck for more detailed study because I believe they represent the most significant tendencies in American fiction during the last fifteen years. Wolfe was an uncompromising individualist, whereas Steinbeck is decidedly social minded. Wolfe belongs to the South and East, Steinbeck to the West Coast; neither, however, is strictly a regionalist. In these and other ways the two writers are different, yet both are distinctively American.

Thomas Wolfe was born in 1900, at Asheville, North Carolina. After graduating from the University of North Carolina he studied in the graduate school of Harvard and taught English in New York University. After a short career of frenzied reading, writing, and traveling, he died, in September, 1938, two weeks before his thirty-eighth birthday. He is the author of four complete novels, two of them published after his death, besides numerous short stories and sketches and a posthumous novel fragment. The four novels are *Look Homeward, Angel* (1929), *Of Time and the River* (1935), *The Web and the Rock* (1939), and *You Can't Go Home Again* (1940). The principal character of the first two is named

Eugene Gant, and the principal character of the last two is named George Webber, but they are both essentially the same personality, and that personality is Thomas Wolfe himself. The four novels together constitute an auto-biography, although the incidents of the story are often modified and sometimes purely imaginary. I shall not undertake to summarize the story, which requires more than three thousand printed pages for Wolfe to tell. It is an account of a man's life from birth through youth to full maturity at about the age of thirty-five. But I will com-ment upon the hero's personality and indicate some of the steps in his mind's development.

In 1936 Wolfe published *The Story of a Novel*, which tells us his experience as a writer and throws light on the meaning of his entire series of novels. In this book he says it is his belief that the deepest search in human life, and the thing that is central in all living, is man's search for a father, not merely the father of his flesh, not merely the lost father of his youth, but the image of a strength and wisdom external to his need and superior to his hunger, to which he can unite the belief and power of his own life. The novels are four episodes in this search.

Look Homeward, Angel tells the story of Eugene Gant's childhood and youth amidst a family to whom he feels more and more alien yet held irrevocably as in a web. He is a very sensitive child, and he recoils alike from the drunken violence of his father and the miserliness of his mother. No one understands him, not even his brother Ben, who is his champion in all family squabbles. But Ben dies while Eugene is still in college, and then the boy knows that he is alone in the world. As he sits in grief with his mother, the bright spirit within him keeps telling him that he is alone and that he must escape. "Go find yourself, lost boy," it says, "beyond the hills."

Wolfe's second novel, *Of Time and the River,* is the record of Eugene's wanderings in search of his lost self. This was a vain search, as he might have known, for before he left his home town to go to New York he had a vision and seemed to speak with Ben's ghost. He calls upon Ben to tell him where he may find the world that will satisfy his hunger and release his imprisoned soul. "Where, Ben?" he cries. "Where is the world?" "Nowhere," Ben's ghost seems to say. "*You* are your world." But Eugene forgets Ben's ghost and pursues his quest. He wants to read all the books in the Harvard library, to visit all the countries and cities of the world, to look deep into the eyes of the millions of New York City and read their innermost secrets. Ten years he must wander, says the author, without rest from hunger, and without satisfaction in the end. Everywhere he went he was alone, and the greater the crowd of people about him, the more alone he was.

To describe those ten years it needed two huge books and part of a third. At the end of *Of Time and the River* he meets the woman whom he is to love. In Wolfe's third book, *The Web and the Rock,* he changes the name of his hero to George Webber, alters his appearance, and retells the story of his childhood with different incidents. This is finished midway in the book, and the last part takes up the story where it was left at the end of the preceding novel. *The Web and the Rock* is concerned largely with the composition and publication of George Webber's first novel, which, of course, is no other than Wolfe's *Look Homeward, Angel.* Foxhall Edwards became George's publisher and friend, without whose advice and firmness he would never have been able to reduce his enormous mass of manuscripts to the form of a novel.

In his last novel, *You Can't Go Home Again*, Wolfe's hero, who is of course to be identified spiritually with the author, satisfies his hunger and completes his search by discovering that the father he seeks is his true self. It was George Webber's friendship with Foxhall Edwards that made it possible. Wolfe writes of the relationship:

> *The older man was not merely friend but father to the younger. Webber, the hot-blooded Southerner, with his large capacity for sentiment and affection, had lost his own father many years before and now had found a substitute in Edwards. And Edwards, the reserved New Englander, with his deep sense of family and inheritance, had always wanted a son but had had five daughters, and as time went on he made of George a kind of foster son. Thus each, without quite knowing that he did it, performed an act of spiritual adoption.*

But Wolfe's hero goes beyond Foxhall Edwards at last. Just as at the end of *Look Homeward, Angel* he had outgrown his family and had cut loose from them, so now he must pass beyond the very man that had helped him to find himself. Foxhall Edwards was like Ecclesiastes, who knows that all is vanity but says, "Don't whine, and don't repine, but *get work done.*" Ecclesiastes did not suffice for George Webber, not any more. He had faith in himself and would not stop until he had found the truth and revealed it. He was not one of the so-called "lost generation," and he was not ambitious for fame. He had seen that fame never satisfied, that nothing would satisfy but truth. When he parted company with his old editor and friend he wrote him a long letter explaining his own beliefs, declaring that he was not a fatalist but a man of faith. "And the essence of all faith, it seems to me, for such a man as I," he wrote, "the essence of religion for people of my belief, is that man's life can be, and will be, better; that man's greatest enemies, in the forms in which they now exist—the forms we see on every hand of fear, hatred, slavery, cruelty, poverty, and need—can be conquered and destroyed." This is a magnificent affirmation of faith, and of course it is the affirmation of Thomas Wolfe as well as of George Webber.

George Webber also said in his letter to Foxhall Edwards that to conquer these enemies of mankind a great and prolonged struggle will be required involving the complete revision of the structure of society as we know it. He did not suggest what the nature of this revision should be. Earlier in the book he had denounced fascism, national socialism, and communism, and even if he had not specifically repudiated these systems we should know that he could never endorse them. It is also clear from the very title of the book that he discarded any notion that we might recover some happier way of life that once prevailed in America. No, America must make a new way, but the new way will be an American way and will embody American ideals. That his plan is a democratic plan is revealed in this statement in the same novel: "So, then, to every man his chance—to every man, regardless of his birth, his shining, golden opportunity—to every man the right to live, to work, to be himself, and to become whatever thing his manhood and his vision can combine to make him—this, seeker, is the promise of America." I do not know where in contemporary literature can be found a clearer statement than Wolfe's of the idealism of Emerson and Whitman as it may be adapted to the conditions of the twentieth century.

Thomas Wolfe never subordinated his art to purposes of propaganda. If he had lived longer he might have written something intended to hasten that revision of the social structure which he said was necessary, but it is not probable that he would ever have been a partisan. Whitman called for poet-prophets able to enlarge men's vision of life, deepen their feelings, and hearten their faith. Of all contemporary writers, Wolfe comes nearest to Whitman's ideal of the large-souled and all-absorbing caresser of life, the loose-tongued sayer, who should become the spokesman for democratic America. When he died he was but a year older than Whitman was when he published the first edition of *Leaves of Grass*. What he might have grown to, it is idle to speculate, but it is a great loss to American literature that he should have died almost as soon as he had won self-mastery and mastery of his craft.

In recent years a number of novels and plays have gone out of their way, more or less, to champion the cause of the unemployed, the poor, and the working class in general. Some of the authors of these novels and plays may have taken a partisan view and thus turned their product into propaganda. Others, however, although moved by genuine sympathy for the masses and believing them mistreated, have handled their subject impartially and with the aim first of all of creating a work of art that should be true and valuable in itself. Among the most successful of these is John Steinbeck. A native of California, born in 1902, Steinbeck has had a great deal of first-hand experience with the problems of itinerant laborers in California orchards and cotton fields. Three of his later books have dealt with these problems.

In Dubious Battle (1936) is the story of a strike by underpaid apple pickers in a California orchard, and of Jim and Mac, two communist agitators who help the workers organize their strike. The communists are interesting primarily as individuals, and although the author describes them with sympathy, he does not attempt to conceal the fact that they act from mingled motives of love of man and love of a fight for the fight's sake. Steinbeck's primary purpose, aside from his purely artistic objectives, is to improve living conditions of the underprivileged classes by assuring them the right to work and earn a living wage. One feels that it is only as aids to this end that labor organizations and communism make any appeal to him. He approves of their professed aims; he does not necessarily approve of their methods.

Steinbeck's next book, *Of Mice and Men* (1937), is a short and classically simple tale of two men who go to work on a California ranch and hope to save enough money to buy a few acres of their own to which they may retire and live as they have dreamed of living. One man is small but intelligent, and he becomes the adviser and protector of the other, who is a huge half-wit with a physical strength that breaks bones without his being conscious of exerting himself. The story ends tragically when the half-wit becomes excited and unintentionally kills a girl who is flirting with him. To save the poor half-wit from being mobbed, his partner shoots him. There is pathos in the strange friendship of these two men and in their passion for owning a bit of earth which they can call home.

Steinbeck's most successful work to date in this kind is *The Grapes of Wrath* (1939), the story of the Joad family in their migration from Oklahoma to California. It is a kind of epic without an individual hero, the real hero being the same as in Carl Sandburg's poems, the people. The Joads had owned land in Oklahoma in early years, but it had been mortgaged and finally lost to absentee capitalists. They were allowed to cultivate the land as tenants, however, until the development of the tractor, which at last made it possible for one man to cultivate as many acres as ten had cultivated before. So the Joads sold their furniture, bought an old truck, and started for California, where they had heard there was plenty of work to be had. I will not repeat this story; most people know it already, either from reading the book or seeing the motion picture made from it. It is sufficient to recall that many tragic events mark their journey, and some pleasant ones, particularly the fellowship with other dispossessed farmers like themselves seeking a new life in the West. When they arrive in California, they discover that there are two or three workers for each job, and the wages consequently fall to lower and lower levels. The police and county officials are in league against them and drive them from county to county. At the end of the story the family is broken up, and all are worse off than they were when they started.

Although nothing is settled, the author has given us a moving account of the sufferings of the migrant laborers of the West and Southwest, and he has also given us a warning that unless something is done to relieve their sufferings and re-establish them as stable members of the social order, their unrest will certainly grow into revolution. Steinbeck blames our social order for the unfortunate plight of these dispossessed people; he does not specify the remedy, but he tries to convince us that a remedy must be found, and quickly. We must get at the causes of these troubles. He says in this book:

The causes lie deep and simply—the causes are a hunger in a stomach, multiplied a million times; a hunger in a single soul, hunger for joy and some security, multiplied a million times; muscles and mind aching to grow, to work, to create, multiplied a million times. The last clear definite function of man—muscles aching to work, minds aching to create beyond the single need—this is man. To build a wall, to build a house, a dam, and in the wall and house and dam to put something of Manself, and to Manself take back something of the wall, the house, the dam; to take hard muscles from the lifting, to take the clear lines and form from conceiving. For man, unlike any other thing organic or inorganic in the universe, grows beyond his work, walks up the stairs of his concepts, emerges ahead of his accomplishments. This you may say of man—when theories change and crash, when schools, philosophies, when narrow dark alleys of thought, national, religious, economic, grow and disintegrate, man reaches, stumbles forward, painfully, mistakenly sometimes. Having stepped forward, he may slip back, but only half a step, never the full step back. This you may say and know it and know it. This you may know when the bombs plummet out of the black planes on the market place, when prisoners are stuck like pigs, when the crushed bodies drain filthily in the dust. You may know it in this way. If the step were not being taken, if the stumbling-forward ache were not alive, the bombs would not fall, the throats would not be cut. Fear the time when the bombs stop falling while the bombers live—for every bomb is proof that the spirit has not died. And fear the time when the strikes stop while the great owners live—for every little beaten strike is proof that the step is being taken. And this you can know—fear the time when Manself will not suffer and die for a concept, for this one quality is the foundation of Manself, and this one quality is man, distinctive in the universe.

This is Steinbeck's social philosophy, and it is essentially the same as that of Thomas Wolfe. It is also, I believe, essentially the social philosophy of Whitman and Emerson and Jefferson. These early Americans would place more emphasis upon the individual as compared with the group, and Emerson and Whitman, and perhaps Jefferson also, would stress moral values more than Steinbeck seems to do. But they all believe that man goes forward, that in his periods of rapid advance he seizes more than he can hold, and hence slips back and loses what he thought he had gained—some of it, but not all—and that his progress is always one of struggle against stubborn opposition.

Steinbeck's philosophy of man's spiritual nature is also somewhat like that of Emerson and Whitman. The preacher, Casy, is his spokesman for the soul. Casy is a sort of transcendentalist, although he would not understand the term. Says Preacher Casy:

I figgered about the Holy Sperit and the Jesus road. I

figgered, "Why do we got to hang it on God or Jesus? Maybe," I figgered, "maybe it's all men an' women we love; maybe that's the Holy Sperit—the human sperit— the whole shebang. Maybe all men got one big soul ever'- body's part of." Now I sat there thinkin' it, an' all of a suddent—I knew it. I knew it so deep down that it was true, and I still know it.

What Casy has discovered is what Emerson called the Over-Soul, and he discovered it, like Emerson, by intui- tion. Like Emerson, too, having been a preacher, he be- came unorthodox and decided not to preach any more, but found it hard to quit.

This conception of the universal soul suggests to Casy that men should work together instead of one against an- other. Says he:

An' I got thinkin', on'y it wasn't thinkin', it was deeper down than thinkin'. I got thinkin' how we was holy when it was one thing. An' it on'y got unholy when one mis'able little fella got the bit in his teeth an' run off his own way, kickin' an' draggin' an' fightin'. Fella like that bust the holiness. But when they're all workin' together, not one fella for another fella, but one fella kind of harnessed to the whole shebang—that's right, that's holy.

Whether Casy is speaking for the author I cannot say, nor can I tell for certain whether he is talking of the fall of man or of the identity of the individual with the uni- versal. As a matter of fact it sounds very much like social- ism. As I said before, Steinbeck differs from Emerson and Whitman, and perhaps also from Thomas Wolfe, in sub- ordinating the individual to the group. But they are all at one in their faith in man's power to rise above circumstances and advance towards the ideal. One type of American thinks power is in the individual and is exercised for the benefit of the group; the other thinks power is in the group and is exercised for the benefit of the individual. These are different points of view and they involve different methods, but at the heart of both philosophies lies the same idealism, faith in human nature, and that idealism is the source of the power.

This revival of Emersonian transcendentalism among the crude and illiterate people of Steinbeck's novel, if it can be taken seriously, is interesting and significant. We might reasonably expect idealism in poetry and among persons who have had cultural advantages. But here is an outcropping of idealism at the lowest economic and cultural level of society. The tendency of the school of naturalism in fiction, to which Steinbeck is closely related, is to look only on the dark side of life, never on the bright side. It is encouraging, therefore, to find naturalism existing cheek by jowl, not only with social idealism and optimism, but with transcendentalism itself.

There is one aspect of Steinbeck's novel that is disturbing, however, and that is the apparent complacency with which he contemplates the mental and moral poverty of his people. He seems to be concerned only with their physical comfort, not at all with the health of their minds and souls. I know the usual reply to this criticism: How can a person cultivate his mind when his body is starved and without shelter? Nevertheless, the criticism is sound. People have been hungry and unhoused before now, and sometimes they have maintained spiritual health even in such adversity. All of the people who are characters in this book are not hungry and cold, but all have the same lack of pride and lack of moral sensitiveness, Casy included. Among all these people, surely there should be a few who have regard for what used to be called decency in their conduct and in their language. I have the same misgiving about some of the works of other contemporary novelists of the school of naturalism. However, I do not believe Americans are as nasty as our novelists make them appear; rather do I think that both writers and readers are afflicted with what James Truslow Adams has called "the mucker pose." Through some strange perversity, we want to appear worse than we are.

Steinbeck's latest novel, *The Moon Is Down* (1942), is of a very different character. In this new book the author's emphasis is upon the spiritual qualities of individuals rather than upon social and economic problems. The difference is only partly accounted for by the fact that the setting and characters of the new book are not American; there is a difference also in the point of view. The theme of the story is that a people who have been accustomed to freedom and democratic institutions will not and cannot be conquered; and though it is obvious that the outward events occur in a town in Norway under German occupation, the author wishes us to understand that the application is universal. The book becomes, therefore, an affirmation of the author's faith in the dignity and worth of human nature and of his belief in the social value of democracy. In his style he has achieved a classic grace and restraint that are rare in contemporary writing. *The Moon Is Down* is Mr. Steinbeck's most brilliant achievement, and it is a further proof of his ability to adapt his genius to the mood of the moment without sacrificing the permanent values of his art.

IX

Robinson and Frost

THE LAST FORTY YEARS OF
the nineteenth century were lean years in the production
of poetry. To be sure, Whitman did some of his best writing in the first part of that period, and Longfellow and
some of his contemporaries were still active. But none of
the younger writers except Emily Dickinson and Sidney
Lanier wrote enduring verse. By comparison, the first
forty years of the twentieth century have been rich in
poetry. In quantity, and perhaps also in quality, the poetry
of these four decades is comparable to that which made the
forty years between 1820 and 1860 the "Golden Day" in
American literature. Several of the first generation of
poets outlived the second and were just coming to the
end of their long career in the last decade of the century,
when the first of the new generation were beginning to
find their voices. In this decade the outlook for American
poetry was darker than it had ever been in the hundred
years of our national existence.

There was no movement in poetry corresponding to
the evolution of fiction from realism to naturalism. The
new generation of poets, although keenly alive to recent
developments in science and philosophy, were men of
strong faith and independent mind and were not over-
whelmed by the tides of materialism that surged about

them. Being idealists and men of principle, they refused to yield to the temptation of popular applause and pecuniary profit; consequently they had to wait through many difficult years for the recognition they deserved.

William Vaughn Moody was the first of the new poets to do effective work. He was born in Indiana in 1869, and died in 1910, before the forces that were bringing about a change in American poetry had been strongly felt. He was really a transition figure, a link between the old and the new. He was educated at Harvard, and afterwards went to teach in the University of Chicago; he therefore had ties both with New England and with the Middle West. In New York he counted among his friends Edwin Arlington Robinson and Percy MacKaye, whose plays *The Canterbury Pilgrims* (1903) and *Jeanne D'Arc* (1906) were among the most successful literary dramas of the time. Moody himself wrote two successful stage plays, *The Great Divide* (1906) and *The Faith Healer* (1909), both of which reflect the author's ideals. But his idealism is to be found chiefly in his poetic dramas, *The Masque of Judgment* (1900), *The Fire-Bringer* (1904), and the fragmentary *Death of Eve*. These poetic dramas deal with the epic struggle of the human spirit to free itself from the shackles of superstition and realize its ideal of perfection. As one critic has put it, he attempted not only, with Milton, to justify the ways of God to man, but also to justify the ways of man to God. His use of the Promethean myth suggests a kinship with Shelley, but in his conception of the unity of God and nature and in his moral idealism he resembles Emerson. He accepted evolution enthusiastically, but understood it as the realization of a sure purpose. In the half-humorous poem "The

Menagerie" he expresses a view of evolution which was seriously believed in:

> *Yes, in the dim brain of the jellied fish*
> *That is and is not living—moved and stirred*
> *From the beginning a mysterious wish,*
> *A vision, a command, a fatal Word:*
> *The name of Man was uttered, and they heard.*

In the justly famous poem "Gloucester Moors" he shows his concern for social injustice by representing the world as a slave ship whose slaves in the hold are the world's poor and whose officers and sailors are the rich and middle classes. It is obvious, therefore, that Moody was sympathetic with science and with social reform, but that he did not permit this sympathy to alienate him from the moral idealism that had become traditional in American poetry.

Edwin Arlington Robinson, a native of Maine, was of the same age as Moody, but his development as a poet was much slower. On account of reverses in the family fortunes, he had to leave Harvard before taking his degree. Deprived of other means of support, he worked when he had to and starved the rest of the time, for he learned that he could not write poetry when he had a regular job, and he had to write poetry. The largest and best portion of his literary work was done after he had passed the age at which Moody had died. He was not deeply moved by the so-called "poetic renaissance" of 1912 to 1915; on the contrary, he had in many ways anticipated it, and in the last decade of the nineteenth century was writing verse that twenty years later was as fresh as the current magazines. He wrote steadily and with a single-

ness of purpose without parallel in our literature before
him except in the single case of Walt Whitman. At his
death in 1935 he had written a body of poetry which in
the complete edition fills fifteen hundred printed pages.
When the high quality of most of his verse is taken into
account, as well as the quantity, it is difficult to see how
he can be denied first rank among American poets of the
twentieth century to this date.

The primary fact to be considered in the study of
Robinson is his search for truth. He gives us pictures of
man torn between faith in his essential divinity and knowledge of his substantial animalism. If he knew more, reason might confirm his wavering faith; if he knew less, he
might be content to dwell in the world of his illusions.
To evade knowledge is despicable; to seek it, dangerous
and sometimes disastrous. The great majority of people
find their moral strength unequal to the demands of
truth, and sink back into their world of illusions, where
they pursue dim phantoms instead of realities and never
truly know themselves. Some who are bold but not strong
face the truth and are destroyed by it. Only the strong and
courageous few, the wise and the good, can face reality
and conquer it. These are the leaders of men whose function it is to draw others into the world of truth-speaking
things. In one sense, therefore, Robinson was not a democrat. The few must save the many, he said, or the many
will be lost. But these few must be stern demanders and
not lavish promisers, and the many must learn the wisdom to choose the hard way to truth instead of the easy
way to folly. Robinson believed with Whitman and
Emerson that every man has in some degree an intuition
of truth, but he was certain that in most men it is an in-

sufficient guide because its power is little whereas the power of illusion and of desire is great. The few in whom the intuition of truth is stronger, and especially those in whom it is reinforced by rational intelligence, must devote themselves to the establishment of those truths which they are given to know and by their precept and example draw the many toward a recognition of their own intuitive revelations.

But truth can be a dangerous thing when known too soon or too late, especially for those whose moral strength is not great. Like Socrates, Robinson teaches self-knowledge, but he warns us not to expect to be flattered. Many of Robinson's poems tell the tragic stories of people who gained self-knowledge too soon or too late and came to destruction thereby. For example, there is Richard Cory, who went home one day and put a bullet through his head; and there is Tasker Norcross, who discovered that his life was empty and could not endure the knowledge of that emptiness. In the long allegorical poem *Amaranth* there is a mysterious character who wanders through human lives, and every man who looks directly into his eyes sees himself as he really is. Many look and forthwith commit suicide, like Richard Cory. Others know Amaranth but are afraid to look into his eyes, preferring to live in a world of illusions. He who faces the truth rashly and dies is a tragic figure, but he who evades the truth is despicable. This is a hard choice that Robinson offers, for only the strong can face their real selves without quailing. One character in this poem is strong. He thinks he is an artist, but when he looks into the eyes of Amaranth he sees that he is not an artist, but is qualified to make pumps successfully. For him also the choice is hard, but he makes it, gives up his palette and brush, and devotes himself to the making of pumps.

In the eyes of the world, no doubt, this pump-maker would be considered a failure, but Robinson did not consider him so. The entire question of success and failure interested Robinson. He shows us that a man fails only when he turns his back on truth and lives in a world of illusions. The earliest of Robinson's long poems, *Captain Craig,* is the story of a man who, in the eyes of the world, was a complete failure, but whose life nevertheless was rich in wisdom and beauty. Captain Craig learned that failure is of the flesh, not of the spirit, and that humanity gains more by the so-called failure of individual men than it gains by their worldly success. You must know, he earnestly assured his young friends,

> *That far above you, for you, and within you,*
> *There burns and shines and lives, unwavering*
> *And always yours, the truth.*

Robinson would say to us through Tasker Norcross, who was what the world calls a success, and through Captain Craig, who was what the world calls a failure, that nothing finally matters in the life of man but truth: truth to himself in the realization of that ideal self which abides within him, and truth to his fellow-men in the dedication of his powers to the creation of that ideal world which is latent in the world we know.

By what ways is the ideal self unfolded, and by what processes is the ideal world created? Robinson devotes a number of long poems to the answering of each of these questions, but I shall cite only one for each. One of Robinson's most powerful studies of individual character is the poem *Matthias at the Door*, first published in 1931. When the story opens Matthias is a successful business man of about fifty years. His wife, Natalie, to whom he has been married many years, is a beautiful woman and he is proud of her accomplishments, but he has never really known her. He has two friends. Garth is a competitor in business who has failed as steadily as Matthias has succeeded. Timberlake, his other friend, was a competitor in love until one day Matthias saved him from a burning house, after which, in gratitude, he left the country so that Matthias could marry Natalie unopposed. That was twenty years before. Now tragic consequences begin to appear. Garth commits suicide, and Matthias feels somehow to blame. Then Timberlake returns, and Natalie and he revive their passion for one another, which both supposed had been forgotten. The inevitable scene occurs in which Matthias discovers their love. Again Timberlake goes away, but neither Matthias nor Natalie can return to the old way of living. Within a short time Natalie commits suicide. Several months afterwards Timberlake returns ill, and Matthias takes him into his house, and the two men have long talks about their tangled lives. Once Timberlake says to Matthias:

> *We are like stairs*
> *For one another's climbing, and are never*
> *Quite told which way it is that we are going*
> *While we are climbing higher, or think we are.*
> *I have not always thought so; but you have,*
> *Matthias, and I have watched you going up*
> *While you were going down. You are down now*

> *As far as you will go—if you remember*
> *That you are like a book with pages in it*
> *You have not read, and cannot read in the dark.*

But Matthias has no light yet to read the hidden page, and he continues to go down. After Timberlake's death his lonely and empty life seems unbearable, and he is about to follow Garth and Natalie through the dark door when suddenly the light dawns within him, he reads the hidden page, and then he knows that he cannot die yet. A voice is speaking to him and it sounds like Garth's voice:

> *We are prisoners now and pupils in a school*
> *Where often our best rewards appear to us*
> *To be our punishments. There's no escape.*
> *To sleep with earth between you and the sun*
> *Is not escape from earth, or from the sun.*
> *It seems a mystery that so many should live*
> *Who are not born, but that's the infinite way,*
> *And one that is not altered or improved*
> *By protest or denial, or by rebellion.*

And so, when the voice is silent, Matthias turns from his dark purpose and goes back to begin life over. Then the poet says:

> *He must go back again; he must be born,*
> *And then must live; and he who had been always*
> *So promptly served, and was to be a servant,*
> *Must now be of some use in a new world*
> *That Timberlake and Garth and Natalie*
> *Had strangely lived and died to find for him.*

Thus through some inscrutable purpose in the universe three out of the four die for the teaching of the remaining one, apparently not the most deserving, who is to be reborn for more effectual living. Robinson would have us know that life is filled with pain and sadness and failure, but not futility; for though many go down to defeat, eventually one will succeed and draw humanity a little farther along the difficult path which leads to the realization of dreams. Man is a learning animal, though not a precocious one, and he will endure a thousand failures before he enjoys a single success, but the comforting fact is that he will endure, and that success will eventually crown his efforts. Robinson offers us hope, not despair, for the future of mankind.

In his last poem, *King Jasper*, which was completed during his final illness, Robinson presents in allegory the tragic story of social revolution. As *Matthias at the Door* describes a crisis in the evolution of an individual, *King Jasper* describes a crisis in the evolution of a civilization. There are six characters. They are Jasper senior, called the King; Jasper junior, his son, called the Prince; Honoria, wife of Jasper senior and mother of Jasper junior, called the Queen; Hebron senior, an inventor, who died many years before the time of this story; Hebron junior, son of Hebron senior, a revolutionist; and finally Zoë, a beautiful young woman of uncertain origin and mysterious powers, who loves Jasper junior and is living with him as his wife although they are not married.

When they were young men the elder Jasper and the elder Hebron were friends and business associates. In some way not altogether creditable, Jasper benefited by Hebron's genius and became rich and powerful while

Hebron remained poor and finally died from the want of things that money could have provided. Although Jasper knew Hebron was dying, he would not save him because he wished to have the fruits of Hebron's genius to increase his own wealth and power. After many years, young Jasper, a rather wild youth, returns home and brings Zoë with him. Honoria, his mother, refuses to be reconciled to her, but his father receives her as his daughter. The Queen is troubled by an intuitive sense of impending doom, and the King knows that subversive forces are at work to undermine his power, which is represented in the poem by factory chimneys. About this time young Hebron returns after many years spent abroad and is seen by young Jasper among his father's chimneys, evidently there with no good purpose, and presently he pays King Jasper a visit. Honoria becomes more and more depressed and finally commits suicide. King Jasper, after a severe illness, is convalescing when the revolution breaks out. He dies from what appears to have been a stroke of paralysis or a heart attack, and soon afterward young Hebron enters his palace and shoots young Jasper through the head. Hebron tries to embrace Zoë, but she kills him with a knife and escapes from the house just before it is blown up by a bomb.

The meaning of the allegory is clear. King Jasper is the representative of power in a capitalistic society, and Honoria is the representative of tradition. The elder Hebron represents individual initiative in a capitalistic society, which is sacrificed to corporate and inhuman power. These are the older generation. Of the younger generation, young Jasper represents the young liberals among the privileged classes who have had the leisure to

devote themselves to other things besides business and
have enjoyed the indulgence of their elders. Young
Hebron represents the intellectuals to whom initiative
is now denied and who seek revenge for their wrongs by
embracing revolutionary ideas. Robinson probably has in
mind either communism or fascism, or both. Zoë is rather
complex and a little mysterious. She undoubtedly represents beauty, including the arts of all kinds, but she also
represents truth, or knowledge, and the spirit of change.
She calls King Jasper father, but we learn in conclusion
that he is her father only in the sense that the growth of
material wealth and power in the capitalistic state fosters
the growth of knowledge and the arts and necessitates the
advent of change. Honoria cannot love Zoë any more
than tradition can welcome change. King Jasper loves
Zoë, but he also fears her, as power must fear change.
She carries a knife, which is truth, and he who feels its
edge knows both himself and the world as before he could
not know them. King Jasper is struck by the knife in a
dream, and wakes to find that knowledge has come to him,
but it has come too late to save him from the forces of
destruction that his ignorance and evil have produced.
Young Hebron dies by this same knife, but before he ex-
pires he too is given to know himself and Zoë, but he is
one who, if he had lived, would not have known, or knowing, would have soon forgotten. Young Jasper found himself in loving Zoë without feeling the knife, and for a
time both he and Zoë believed that they might outlive
the revolution and reshape the world with knowledge and
beauty. But young Jasper was, as they learned, still inseparably bound by nature to the old order and has to die
with it. Only Zoë would live on, but she must live alone.

The philosophical meaning of this poem is much the same as that of *Amaranth*, discussed earlier in this chapter. The world is forever changing, sometimes peacefully, but more often in struggle and revolution. The motives that lead to change are varied, including ignorance, evil, hate, but also knowledge, beauty, love. Ignorance is characteristic of the many, knowledge of the few, and those rare ones who possess knowledge, like Zoë, are doomed to a lonely wayfaring life. Knowledge came to King Jasper, but too late. His son tells him that kings could teach the masses better than revolutionaries like Hebron if they could see "an inch or two ahead of them." That is to say, revolutions could be avoided if the evils that breed them could be seen by men in power before it is too late.

It is clear that Robinson saw dangers of world revolution in 1935 while he was writing this poem, but he was not altogether pessimistic. His vision of social evolution is probably set forth in a speech by Zoë in reply to King Jasper's remark that "there would be no kings if there were none to suffer."

>   *"There might be,"*
> *Zoë said, smiling. "We should all be kings,*
> *Or queens, if we could see ourselves in others.*
> *But that's a long, long way from where we are;*
> *And a few suffocatings and blood-drenchings*
> *Of helpless heroes who will not know why,*
> *Or what it means, will show the devil's ahead,*
> *With banners and with music of all nations.*
> *The devil is an impartial patriot,*
> *Unprejudiced as he is promiscuous.*
> *Today the devil is more than God. Tomorrow*

He will be more, and more. Out of it all
He'll come with crutches, and not the devil he was.
Father, don't ask me when, for I don't know."

The devil draws men apart; Christ draws them together. Robinson understood as well as Whitman that only when we can see ourselves in others in love and brotherhood can we expect the full and free development of the individual and a peaceful and harmonious organization of society. Whitman believed that this end might be consummated with less suffering and in less time than Robinson foresaw, but their faith is equally sure. Robinson tells us the worst that is to come as well as the best in the belief that truth, though it may destroy many, will save a few, and in saving a few will at last save all.

The second great New England poet of our century is Robert Frost. Frost was actually born in San Francisco, in 1875, and lived the first ten years of his life in that city. In his early middle age he lived in England for two years, and published there his first book of poems. Since then he has traveled much and lived for brief periods in many different places. But wherever he goes, he takes the quality of New England with him, and wherever his poems are read, there will be found the people and the fields and mountains of New England. Robinson's studies of character are formal portraits that stand out vividly against blurred settings, whereas Frost's are informal snapshots from everyday life in which the human figures blend with the landscape. Robinson's mood is predominantly sad, Frost's is predominantly cheerful.

Not that Frost was unacquainted with sorrow and mental sickness. Several of his poems picture the tortured lives of lonely people who suffer pain and frustration and the disease of mind and spirit for which there is no cure. In "Home Burial," for example, we are made to feel a mother's horror when she learns that her husband himself dug the grave, which she can see from a window in the house, where their child was buried. This and other poems in *North of Boston* tell of twisted lives, families rotting like the houses they hide in, and old hates and superstitions, relics of the past, housed in the dusty attics of the mind. Less painful is the pathos of the worn-out hired man, whose return to the house of his benefactor to die suggests the thought that home is the place where, when you have to go there, they have to take you in. Frost, like all true poets, understands the value of pain, and failure, and death, and he would have us know that it is not man's accomplishment only that he is to be judged by, but also his aim. This he makes clear for us in the sonnet "A Soldier." Sometimes life's darker side is revealed symbolically in otherwise innocent natural occurrences, though even in the symbolism of nature he never sees man's case as utterly without hope.

More characteristic are moods of tranquil happiness and contentment with the world, both human and natural. Like William Cullen Bryant, Frost was a lover of nature in all seasons, the autumn and winter no less than the spring and summer. The happiness and confidence with which he and his wife, in their youth, undertook a way of life which their families and friends possibly advised against may be reflected in the short poem called "In Neglect."

> *They leave us so to the way we took,*
>> *As two in whom they were proved mistaken,*
> *That we sit sometimes in the wayside nook,*
> *With mischievous, vagrant, seraphic look,*
>> *And* try *if we cannot feel forsaken.*

Not only was his own life, in the main, a happy one, but it seemed to him that the people of America as a whole were happy and fortunate in their lives. Like William James he believes that optimism is good because it makes the world better, and that pessimism is bad because it makes the world worse.

Frost's optimism extends to more than mere cheerfulness. He is a true idealist, believing with Emerson that the ideal is an activating force in human life. He also believes that the utmost that man conceives it possible to become is latent in him already. This is the thought expressed in the first poem of his first volume, *A Boy's Will.* If he should succeed some day in fulfilling his wish to explore the unknown "unto the edge of doom," he says, and if his friends should follow and find him there, they would discover that he was unchanged, only more sure of what he thought was true. He has found that truth is elusive and that it comes to us, when not otherwise accessible, by revelation. But revelation is rare, and often we are in danger of following half-gods, which are false gods. He describes one who was "running with joy" on the trail of a Demon whom he knew to be no true god, when suddenly the Demon rose up from behind him and laughed at him mockingly so that he was ashamed. The true gods do not reveal themselves thus; of them we are vouchsafed a glimpse at rare intervals, but no more. Even

glimpses are reserved only for those who are "not in position to look too close." Once, looking at his reflection in a
well, he thought he saw through and beyond the image
a "something more of the depths," a white, uncertain
something, but it vanished almost as soon as perceived.
This whiteness, this uncertainly perceived truth, which
lies just beyond the known and the perceptible, is the goal
of all our seeing and knowing. It is Frost's faith that we
shall reach this goal eventually in spite of all hindrances.
A tree fallen across the road becomes a symbol of things
which halt but cannot long delay man's progress.

The figure of truth as a light which we see through an
image reflected in water suggests that the object before
us towards which we move is but the image of the reality
which lies behind us, at the source of our lives. In the poem
"West-Running Brook" Frost develops this thought. A
man and a woman are watching a wave in the running
brook where it strikes an obstruction and turns back upon
itself in a wave of white water. The man says:

> "Speaking of contraries, see how the brook
> In that white wave runs counter to itself.
> It is from that in water we were from
> Long, long before we were from any creature.
> Here we, in our impatience of the steps,
> Get back to the beginning of beginnings,
> The stream of everything that runs away.
> Some say existence like a Pirouot
> And Pirouette, forever in one place,
> Stands still and dances, but it runs away,
> It seriously, sadly, runs away
> To fill the abyss' void with emptiness.

It flows beside us in this water brook,
But it flows over us. It flows between us
To separate us for a panic moment.
It flows between us, over us, and with *us.*
And it is time, strength, tone, light, life and love—
And even substance lapsing unsubstantial;
The universal cataract of death
That spends to nothingness—and unresisted,
Save by some strange resistance in itself,
Not just a swerving, but a throwing back,
As if regret were in it and were sacred.
It has this throwing backward on itself
So that the fall of most of it is always
Raising a little, sending up a little.
Our life runs down in sending up the clock.
The brook runs down in sending up our life.
The sun runs down in sending up the brook.
And there is something sending up the sun.
It is this backward motion toward the source,
Against the stream, that most we see ourselves in,
The tribute of the current to the source.
It is from this in nature we are from.
It is most us."

I have quoted at length from this poem because it so aptly expresses Frost's philosophy of idealism in harmony with the facts of science. Man is not merely a part of the flowing stream of things; he is that, but he is that contrary something which the stream produces but which reverses the general downward movement and returns towards its source. If then the mind is a product of material evolution, it is like that white wave in the brook which mysteri-

ously faces backward towards its source. The mind shows
its kinship to God by the exercise of an independent will
that counteracts the stream from which it rises and does
not follow that stream into the abyss.

All men have this element in common, and therefore
they have a common good and a common destiny. Frost is
a genuine New Englander, and he has the New Englander's tough individualism, but he has also a sense of the
brotherhood of men and their need for co-operative enterprise. In the poem "The Tuft of Flowers" he shows
how two workmen are brought into a closer harmony of
feeling and action through their common love of flowers.
Early of a morning one laborer had cut the hay and left
it to dry. Later in the day a second laborer came to turn it.
Each had to be alone at his work, and his thought was
that all men must be alone "whether they work together
or apart." But presently his eye, following the flutterings
of a butterfly, discovers a tuft of flowers which had been
spared by the mower, although he had cut all around
them. This common love of the flowers became a bond
between the two men, and henceforth they were not alone.

> *"Men work together," I told him from the heart,*
> *"Whether they work together or apart."*

One might almost fancy that the butterfly had brought
the spirits of the two men together by leading the second
one to notice the flowers left by the scythe of the first. The
idea that there is something in nature that makes for unity
and co-operation rather than for diversity and enmity is
developed in the familiar poem "Mending Wall." New
England farms are separated by stone walls for fences,

and in the spring the farmers on adjoining farms work to-gether in replacing the stones fallen during the winter. One farmer, quoting the traditional saying that he had from his father, says, "Good fences make good neigh-bors." The other farmer, who is the poet, replies, "Some-thing there is that doesn't love a wall, That wants it down." He cannot clearly explain to his neighbor. He could say that the elves did it, and yet that would not do for the unimaginative. The elves did not really throw down the stones in order to bring the two farmers to-gether, any more than the butterfly sought the tuft of flowers to bring the two workmen into spiritual harmony. But it is *as if* they did, and the result is the same either way. "Q. E. D.," says the scientist, and therein lies the sum of his teaching. But the poet looks beyond what is to what might be; his wisdom is in "as if." The butterfly's need for the flower and the man's need are outwardly different and yet essentially the same. There are other passages in Frost's poetry which suggest the kinship if not the iden-tity of instinct in nature and conscious purpose in man.

Of Frost's political and economic views I shall not attempt to report, because they are not clearly indicated in his poems. It is obvious that he is an individualist. Moreover, the people in whom he shows most interest are simple farm men and women of New England, and the spirit in which he presents them is democratic. Some-thing one of his characters says in "The Black Cottage" about the Jeffersonian principle that "all men are created equal" may indicate Frost's belief in democracy and equality as ideals which, though not yet realized, may one day be realized if enough people believe strongly in the possibility of their realization.

But Frost accepts life as he finds it, the good and the bad, and never supposes that one may escape an unpleasant fact by denying the reality of its existence. He does not forget that the ideal, to have value, must be related to the real. Man is of heaven and earth; he must know how to rise above his earthiness, but he must also know when and how to return. He makes the birch tree a symbolic link between the real and the ideal. You may climb the birch tree *toward* heaven, but when the tree can bear you no further, it tips gently and sets you down again upon earth. That, says Frost, is "good both going and coming back." The earth always seems a better place after such an experience. This is the heart of Frost's idealism, to adhere to the real, but to move towards the ideal.

X

Contemporary Radical and Reactionary Poets

A STRICT CLASSIFICATION OF American poets of the twentieth century would be difficult if not impossible, but if one is not particular about minor discrepancies and overlappings a classification for convenience can be made. For the purposes of this study I have found it possible to arrange most of the poets in three groups; namely, the conventional group, including all who adhere, in the main, to traditional forms and whose ideas have evolved without violence from the thought of the past; the radical group, including all who have broken sharply with the past, whether in the form or the content of their verse; and the reactionary group, including all who in one way or another have turned against the present and reverted to something in the past which promises a stable foundation for the human spirit. With the help of this classification I shall attempt to find my way through the maze of contemporary poetry.

Of the conventional poets, the two most important were the principal subjects of the preceding chapter. Compared to Robinson and Frost, all other writers of conventional verse in the twentieth century are of minor importance. Among the older writers, George Sterling went in for high romance and fine rhetoric, Lizette Reese and

Sara Teasdale for graceful sentiment, and John G. Nei-
hardt and Witter Bynner for democracy, the one in narrative and the other in lyric patterns. More intense were
the sonnet sequence *Two Lives*, by William Ellery Leon-
ard, and the lyrics of Elinor Wylie, half personal and half
metaphysical. One of the older poets who has not been
sufficiently appreciated of late years is Anna Hempstead
Branch. Her poetry has a quiet power and a spiritual
quality that are too rare in contemporary writing. Her
epic poem *Nimrod* is her most notable work. All of these
writers were sufficiently mature before the outbreak of
the first World War to escape any serious mental upset.

Prominent among the poets who were somewhat
younger is Edna St. Vincent Millay. She belonged to the
war generation, which was still young and impression-
able when the crash came. The poets of this generation,
finding the Puritan virtues less potent in a war-torn world
than they had been taught to expect, threw them over-
board and clung to the precarious security of sensuous
values, or else abandoned altogether the search for values
and tried to find satisfaction in a flippant cynicism. In recent years Miss Millay has shown signs of accepting a
greater responsibility in fulfilling her poetic office than
in her youth she had been willing to accept. In *Conversation at Midnight* she expresses through her characters,
who are all men, several different views of the state of
human affairs; but the people who hold these views, the
participants in the conversation, are mostly outside the
main stream of things and speak as partisans of untried
theory or as onlookers. The dominant mood, in so far as
one can be felt, is rather pessimistic. Whether this is the
author's mood is uncertain; the author, in fact, seems

lost in the crowd of men who are somehow not quite men. In her sonnet sequence "Epitaph for the Race of Man" she strikes a definitely pessimistic note, but she does leave the doomed human race one consolation, which is that if man is to be destroyed he must destroy himself, being otherwise indestructible.

More recently she has published two volumes, *Huntsman, What Quarry?* (1939) and *Make Bright the Arrows* (1940). These volumes prove that Miss Millay had been deeply stirred by events in Europe during the years immediately preceding their publication and that she was concerned at last for the preservation of that human race which before she had consigned to doom. The second of the volumes was a passionate plea for aid to Britain. The first poem is "To the Maid of Orleans," and calls for a new sacrifice. The last two lines carry the point:

> *Martyred many times must be*
> *Who would keep his country free.*

This is in the mood of Edwin Arlington Robinson and very unlike the moods of Miss Millay's earlier poems. It would hardly be true to say that Miss Millay has thrown off her pessimism altogether, but now that her world faces real tragedy instead of the mere mental sickness of twenty years ago, her strong sense of life will not permit an uncourageous mood. The least that one can say is that her courage implies faith.

Very different is the poetry of Stephen Vincent Benét, in whose ballads are recorded many a lively episode from American history and folklore. His epic, *John Brown's Body,* produced in the late twenties, might have become a landmark in American literature, but it failed to rise to its opportunities. This poem attempts to capture the spirit of the famous martyr and fanatic as it worked through the events of the Civil War, but it succeeds only in giving a series of vivid pictures of that struggle. The poet, it appears, has no wisdom from his experience, and no knowledge beyond the fact that out of John Brown's body has grown the giant and mechanical body of America in the Machine Age. What this mechanical America portends of good or ill the poet does not report.

It is a fact worthy of note that among the younger conventional poets there are few who appear to have been strongly influenced by Robinson and Frost. Somewhat in the manner of Frost is the poetry of Robert P. Tristram Coffin, of Maine. Mr. Coffin is at his best in character sketches of the types of people still to be found in the less traveled parts of New England. He lacks something of Frost's humor and much of his philosophical insight, but his poems, especially his ballads, have a charm peculiar to themselves.

Among those who have written in the manner of Robinson, Mark Van Doren is most worth considering in this study, especially since the publication recently of his long poem, *The Mayfield Deer,* based upon a legend or incident out of Illinois a hundred years ago. It is the story of the victory, after two tragic killings, of love and brotherhood over hate and pride, accomplished in part through the philosophizing of a little Norwegian storekeeper named Thorsten. There is someone in himself, says Thorsten, who is more himself than Thorsten, and who "would be all that is" if it were possible for man to be all. Here is a new outcropping of transcendentalism, but in the manner of the twentieth century. Out of man's limitations grow his tragedies, but with greater understanding he can overcome the limitations and avoid the tragedies. This, which I take to be the meaning of Mr. Van Doren's poem, is very close to the thought which is illustrated over and over in Robinson's narratives. It is comforting to come upon it again in a poem of the year 1942.

The gradual evolution of American poetry was disrupted during the years 1912 to 1920 by revolutionary activities which radical spirits were wont to term the Renaissance in American Poetry, but which a few skeptics have dismissed as a tempest in a teapot. The truth probably lies somewhere between the two extremes. The changes which are to become permanent would no doubt have come in any case, but less promptly. Whether this movement was a tempest in a teapot or a true revolution, its effects have struck wide and deep, and the end of them is not yet to be seen. We know that some good has come of it, and probably some harm has come too; but it is still too soon to pass final judgment.

I have classified as radicals all the poets who became a part of this movement, but there were two very different groups of them. One group was social in its aims and rather democratic; the other was esoteric and aristocratic, in an intellectual and æsthetic sense at least. The social poets were Middle Westerners without literary erudition, and for them communication was an indispensable function of poetry. Poetry was a means by which they hoped to influence people. The esoteric poets were largely influenced by European backgrounds, and many of them found living in Europe more agreeable than living in America. There was a tendency among them to deal with words as a musical composer deals with notes or an artist

with line and color. The coherence of thought ceased to
be a major consideration. Obviously the social poet and
the esoteric poet had little in common.

The founder and first important leader of the esoteric
radicals was the expatriate Ezra Pound. With two or
three others of like mind, he organized the Imagist school
of poetry and got up a set of principles. Every poem, according to his school, must present an image, and an image
was described by Mr. Pound as "that which presents an
intellectual and emotional complex in an instant of time."
This image was to be presented in definite outlines and
without the limitations of rhyme and conventional meter.
Pound soon had many "joiners," not all of whom were
able or willing to follow his strict principles. He was himself too much of an experimenter to be content with a
school, even of his own founding, and presently began to
try other methods. Pound had rebelled against what he
considered American crudeness, Puritanism, and all forms
of conventionality. In his early poetry he acknowledged
the influence of earlier liberal American poets, especially
Whitman, but evidently it was Whitman's sense of freedom and not his humanity or his faith that appealed to
Pound. Pound's retreat to England and finally to Italy
and his absorption, in his later poetry, in medievalism suggest a desire to escape the responsibilities of a modern poet
in America. The complexity of his verse reflects the erudition of the antiquarian more than the social complexity of
a mechanical age. So far as I understand the meaning of
his poetry, it is amoral and undemocratic, and its significance in the present study is therefore chiefly negative.

Associated with Pound in the imagist movement was
H. D. (Hilda Doolittle), whose verse has something of

Hellenic clarity and precision but does not convey a strong sense of life. She has been the most rigidly consistent practitioner of imagist principles, and in so far as her poems fail, they fail because of the principles. The subdued elegance and precision of visual image in the verse of Wallace Stevens suggest the qualities of H. D., but his work has more fullness of body than hers. Marianne Moore has wit and an acute perception of the physical world, but she expects a good deal of her readers in bridging the frequent gaps in her thought sequences. Other poets of this group are John Gould Fletcher, an experimentalist and impressionist who has lately turned to conventional forms; William Carlos Williams, who gives to each poem a distinctive form suited to its requirements; and Amy Lowell, who was both a representative poet and the propagandist for the group in its combative period. Conrad Aiken may be named with these, although his poetry is in a richer style, having many of the qualities of music. Recently he has increased the difficulty of reading his elaborately patterned verse by devoting it to the intricacies of psychoanalysis. With but rare exceptions, the enthusiasm of all these writers is for words, not for ideas or things; consequently their poems have the unsubstantial quality of filigree or delicate soap carvings.

The other branch of the radicals, the social or democratic poets, were less interested in word patterns and more positively interested in people. The most notable exemplars of this school were Edgar Lee Masters, Vachel Lindsay, and Carl Sandburg, all born in the Middle West and all approaching middle age when they achieved success as poets. I have included Masters with Lindsay and Sandburg because, like them, he found his themes in the lives of ordinary American men and women. The best of his poems are included in the volume entitled *Spoon River Anthology* (1915), a collection of epitaphs in which deceased persons are represented as telling the truth about their lives. These poems interpret the lives of ordinary American village people in many phases: fulfillment, futility, disillusionment, irony. The point of view in each poem is determined not by the poet but by the experience of the subject described. The dominant mood of the book is depressing, and yet the lives revealed were by no means all unhappy or ignoble. The poet is coldly impartial, and it may be this impartiality that makes the book seem more pessimistic than it really is.

The mood of Vachel Lindsay's poems, on the other hand, is exuberant and optimistic. The difference between Masters and Lindsay is suggested in the following lines of "The Prairie Battlements," a poem which Lindsay dedicated to Masters, as he says, "with great respect."

> *Here upon the prairie*
> *Is our ancestral hall.*
>
> .   .   .
>
> *Ghouls are in the cellar,*
> *But fays upon the stairs.*

One saw the ghouls mostly, the other the fays. It is not easy to distinguish the genuine poet in Lindsay from the showman, the evangelist, and the reformer. His ultimate object, no doubt, was to make the world over. He thought that a good place to begin would be his native city of Springfield, Illinois. In an introductory statement to his *Collected Poems* he says:

> *I believe that civic ecstasy can be so splendid, so un-*
> *utterably afire, continuing and increasing with such apoc-*
> *alyptic zeal, that the whole visible fabric of the world can*
> *be changed. I believe in a change in the actual fabric, not*
> *a vague new outline. . . . And I say: change not the mass,*
> *but change the fabric of your own soul and your own*
> *visions, and you change all.*

This dream of changing the world through the soul of the individual was to be accomplished by evangelistic means. In his evangelism he used all the tricks of the showman. But he was also a mystic, and in such delicate recreations of a legendary past as the ancient China of "The Chinese Nightingale" he is at his best.

He is most widely known for his religious and patriotic poems. In "General William Booth Enters into Heaven" he pictures the hero's triumphant entry, followed by the poor, the lame, and the criminal whom he has aided. In "The Congo" he gives a dramatic account of the rise of the Negro race from voodoo worship to a higher faith. One of his most interesting poems is that which tells the story of Johnny Appleseed, a legendary character who wandered over the middle western region before its settlement and sowed apple seeds which had grown into bearing trees when the white men came. He becomes a symbol of the American creator.

> *A ballot-box in each apple,*
> *A state capital in each apple,*
> *Great high schools, great colleges,*
> *All America in each apple.*

In "The Santa Fé Trail" a man sits by a milestone on the

highway and watches the United States go by in roaring automobiles, and Lindsay contrasts the aims of the man sitting there with the aims of the travelers in the cars.

> *They are hunting the goals that they understand:—*
> *San-Francisco and the brown sea-sand.*
> *My goal is the mystery the beggars win.*

In his "Litany of the Heroes" he surveys the work of heroes from Moses to Woodrow Wilson, and stresses the influence of the classic spirit, the medieval spirit, the religious spirit, the scientific spirit, and the American spirit. His American heroes are Lincoln, Emerson, Whitman, Theodore Roosevelt, and Woodrow Wilson. He was, of course, an enthusiastic believer in the League of Nations. He praises science as "forerunner of a higher mystic day," and says "Lord, give us Darwin's eyes!"

Lindsay traveled widely and continuously, and everywhere he went he read his poems to whoever would listen. Often he had great audiences, and he read with beauty and power. His poems were made to be read aloud, and when they are read silently they appear trivial and sometimes almost silly. Of all our American poets, Lindsay probably came nearest to speaking the heart and mind of poor and uneducated people. There was something cheering in his faith. It is not too late, he argued, to build our own young land right. "MAN is unborn. Tomorrow he is born."

Like Lindsay, Carl Sandburg is a poet of the people, but he is more robust, more subtle, less sentimental. He has often been compared with Whitman, and rightly so, although he has less genius than Whitman, less power, less wisdom. Sandburg lacks Whitman's cosmic view and his mystic insight, but he makes us more intimately acquainted with the people in the street. He lets them speak for themselves, and he calls them by their first names familiarly. Whitman sacrifices realism for vision; Sandburg sacrifices vision for realism.

Both rebelled against the conventions of poetry, discarding the restrictions of rhyme and meter and accepting all things, the unpleasant as well as the pleasant, as suitable for poetic treatment. Both likewise approved the materialism of America and hoped that it might be good rather than bad in its final effects. Sandburg's first poems shocked many readers, and even yet it is rather startling to come across his enthusiastic poem to Chicago, "Hog Butcher for the World," comparing it to a husky, brawling, wicked fighter, proudly calling it "City of the Big Shoulders." But this is not the whole of Sandburg. Sometimes he is gentle, even tender; and he is the equal of any other in appreciation of the subtle gradations of sound and color and form that go to produce beauty. The noise of the factory, the raucous talk of public places, the lonely sound of wind and rain, the mystery of fog, the peace of death—all these he makes us feel and understand.

He writes well of nature, but he is chiefly interested in people, all kinds of people, not merely the good or clever. For him people are first of all individuals, but they are also nations and races. In his fine poem "Washington Monument by Night" he has created an effective symbol both of Washington the man and of the republic which he founded. He wrote:

> *The stone goes straight.*
> *A lean swimmer dives into night sky,*
> *Into half-moon mist.*

And again:

> *The republic is a dream.*
> *Nothing happens unless first a dream.*

And finally:

> *The name of an iron man goes over the world.*
> *It takes a long time to forget an iron man.*

Carl Sandburg's greatest tribute to the people he loves is his last book, which he has entitled *The People, Yes*. This title in itself places Sandburg among the *yea-sayers* of the world, the affirmers as against the deniers. Although he is an optimist in his outlook for the people, he warns that we must not expect to advance except with labor and pain. He tells about a man who lived for six weeks in a tent set up in front of the Great Sphinx of Egypt. The man said to the Sphinx:

> *"What would you say if I should ask you to*
> *tell me something worth telling?"*
> *And the Sphinx broke its long silence:*
> *"Don't expect too much."*

"The people," says Carl Sandburg, "is a lighted believer and hoper," but, he adds, "the people is a knower too."

> *The people a knower whose knowing grows by*
> *what it feeds on*
> *The people wanting to know more, wanting.*

But he realizes that the people do not learn easily. He makes us feel

> *the pity of men learning by shocks,*
> *By pain and practice,*
> *By plunges and struggles in a bitter pool.*

He describes the people as "mixed from a bowl of sky blue dreams and sea slime facts," and he says that though "man will never arrive, man will be always on the way." He tells this story, long current, of the pioneer who is "holding his own":

> *"I didn't have anything*
> *when I landed here*
> *and I ain't got anything now*
> *but I got some hope left.*
> *I ain't lost hope yet.*
> *I'm a wanter and a hoper."*

Don't expect too much, but go on expecting. That is Sandburg's advice to the people. "Who can fight against the future?" he says, and he means that the future belongs to "the people." "Haven't the people gone on and on always taking more of their own?" Here is a fuller statement of his view of the future:

> *The free man willing to pay and struggle*
> *and die for the freedom for himself and*
> *others*
> *Knowing how far to subject himself to dis-*
> *cipline and obedience for the sake of an*
> *ordered society free from tyrants, ex-*
> *ploiters and legalized frauds—*

This free man is a rare bird and when you
  meet him take a good look at him and
  try to figure him out because
Some day when the United States of the Earth
  gets going and runs smooth and pretty
  there will be more of him than we
  have now.

Lest we should think this freedom will come easily, he reminds us at the close of his poem:

In the darkness with a great bundle of grief
  the people march.

The People, Yes, whatever its shortcomings as a poem, is the authentic voice of America, and its keynote is faith in man's power to build eventually the ideal world that he has dreamed.

All the poets left to be discussed, whom I have grouped together and called reactionary, have one quality in common: they have repudiated, in one fashion or another, their immediate cultural inheritance and their responsibilities as practical citizens, and have escaped into a formal past or into spiritual negation. What moves them is a kind of inverted romanticism. They have become unsentimental and hyper-intellectual. Some of them have been called classicists, but their poetry rarely possesses the classical qualities of simplicity and clarity. They revert to French Symbolists and to the seventeenth-century metaphysical poets for their literary models, but exploit antiquity for materials. With all this reversion to the past, however, they are ultra-modern in their cynicism, their metrical experimentation, and their devotion to the methods of psychoanalysis. Theirs has been called the "cult of unintelligibility" because they sometimes appear to set down as from dictation the loosely associated ideas that float uncontrolled on the stream of consciousness.

The reactionary group has much in common with the esoteric radicals. Indeed, Ezra Pound may be called the foster-father of both schools. Pound was born in Idaho in 1885, educated in the East, and self-exiled to Europe, where he has lived since 1908, first in London and now for many years in Italy. Like Henry James, he found American ways distasteful; but one suspects that he has not been wholly satisfied with the ways of Europe. The most ambitious, though not in all respects the best, of his writings is the long series of *Cantos,* now amounting to seventy or more, which have appeared in several installments through a period of years, and which give no indication of approaching a conclusion.

The second of this group is T. S. Eliot, who was born in 1888, and educated chiefly at Harvard, the Sorbonne, and Oxford. His learning seems to be even greater than Pound's, and he too has been influenced by the new psychology of the unconscious, but he imposes a stricter form upon his verse than Pound. His most influential poem is *The Waste Land,* published in 1922, in which he represents the barrenness of life in the modern age. Without notes or other helps, most readers can derive from this poem no coherent sequence of thought, but none could fail to sense the mood of despair in which it is written. Like Pound, he became dissatisfied with America, and since 1912 he has lived chiefly in England. Some years ago he aligned himself with the Anglican Church and became a British subject. Most of his writing in recent years has been of a critical nature, and he is doubtless one of the most influential literary personages in the twentieth century. His energies have been directed against all modern movements that lead the individual away from established institutions.

His later poems are beautiful formulas of Christian piety, with one important exception, but they give little comfort to those who rest their faith on the efficacy of the individual soul. In *Ash Wednesday* (1930) he renounced the self as will and turned gratefully to the Church for guidance. Later, in *The Rock: a Pageant Play*, he made a strong appeal to the modern man to forsake the dark ways of materialism and follow the light of the spirit. *Murder in the Cathedral* (1935) is a dramatic poem representing the martyrdom of Thomas Becket, Archbishop of Canterbury, as an episode in the unfolding of the immutable will of God. His latest poem, *The Family Reunion* (1939), dramatizes the operation of fate in the social milieu. The Eumenides in this tragedy perform a function comparable to that performed by the assassins of Thomas Becket. In *The Family Reunion* a man who all his life has fled from phantoms, which become real to him only when he reaches what he believes to be his last refuge, at length finds freedom in the determination to pursue his pursuers. In this act of the will there is a suggestion of that power of the spirit over fate which Emerson constantly affirmed. But since Eliot does not reveal the consequences of this act of the will, we cannot know for certain whether it is indeed a free act or merely a disguised link in a chain of fated events. In the absence of more positive evidence of a change in his views, it seems necessary to conclude that Eliot remains a pessimist, with no more faith in human nature than he had when he wrote *The Waste Land.*

In the early nineteen-twenties a group of students and faculty members of Vanderbilt University founded a magazine which they called, significantly, *The Fugitive;* it continued only two or three years, but the founders and their successors have become well known. The most prominent of the Fugitive group were John Crowe Ransom and Allen Tate. Their verse is notable for wit and intellectual virtuosity, and their critical writing for the championship of agrarianism and the culture of the antebellum South. As a poet, Mr. Ransom is outstanding in this group, but even he has only a thin vein of ore to work, and in recent years he has devoted his energies principally to literary criticism and editorial work. In poetry he rarely addresses his subject directly and seriously, preferring the oblique and the satiric approach. His aim is to say things more clever than true, and to evince wit rather than emotion. Allen Tate is more serious but less clear. His object seems to be to state simple things—such as that the moon shines brightly or that the night falls—in as elaborate a way as possible, suggesting by his indirection and elaboration that they mean something important, but by no means allowing his reader to know directly what they mean. Like Pound and Eliot these regionalists (of the past, not the present) scintillate so in their manner that their matter is lost. There is, at best, but an imperfect communication. Thus while they have not abandoned the soil of America, they have scorned to address their contemporaries in a language that can be readily understood. They are avowedly reactionary; indeed Mr. Tate is the author of a book which he calls *Reactionary Essays on Poetry and Ideas.*

These Southerners are definitely unfriendly to the democratic idealism of Emerson and Whitman.

Three other poets who may be said to derive from Pound and Eliot are Archibald MacLeish, Hart Crane, and Horace Gregory. Mr. MacLeish has lately become interested in liberal movements in America and can definitely be said to have broken away from his early tendency to lose himself in metaphysical pyrotechnics. Hart Crane tried in his brief and tragic career to build a philosophical foundation for his life out of American materials. His symbolic poem *The Bridge* is the product of this effort. Taking Brooklyn Bridge as a symbol of the unifying principle in the universe, he extends it to the geography and life of America and then tries to extend it further to the unknown and ideal world, but does not wholly succeed. The poem shows the influence of Whitman, especially of Whitman's "Song of the Open Road" and "Passage to India"; but Crane really had no faith in which to anchor his bridge, and consequently he failed to create a philosophy by which he could live. The third member of this group, Horace Gregory, has had sympathies with communism, and is definitely hopeful in his philosophy though not very confident. Perhaps his most important poem, or series of poems, is *Chorus for Survival* (1935). In this poem, like Crane in *The Bridge*, he embraces the modern spirit and links it with earlier American idealism. Crane looked to Whitman for inspiration, whereas Gregory looked to Emerson. The following lines illustrate the mood of *Chorus for Survival*:

Over the cities and the yellowing plain
In bitter drought:

> wait for new rain, welcome the men
> *Who shall survive, outface despair,*
> *Terror and hate*
> to build new fire
> *At an empty hearth,*
> *Burn doubt and fear.*

The last and in some respects the most important of my group of reactionary poets is Robinson Jeffers, born in 1887, who for many years has lived in seclusion on the west coast of California. Strictly speaking, he does not belong in this group. He returns to Greek sources for some of his materials, and he also adopts the psychology of the subconscious, but his style is clear and his rejection of human ideals is too complete to allow his acceptance of any institution or any culture corrupted by man's meddling. He not only repudiates humanitarianism and democracy, but all forms of religion, Christian or pagan, and rests his hope for man purely on the law of physical nature. He has written a number of long narrative poems depicting the lives of families isolated in the wild country near where he lives. These people live inwardly and develop abnormal habits, usually involving incest, which end in abortion, suicide, and murder. His poems are rich with beautiful and powerful descriptions, but they are also filled with scenes of cruelty, insanity, and horror. In the long poems his philosophy appears in its most unpleasant effects; we must turn to his shorter poems for abstract statements of his views.

His philosophy may be called a pantheistic materialism. God is represented in unconscious nature, and man's conscious separateness is evil. The universe is beautiful in its wholeness, but not in its parts. All that is human, that is, all that seeks to control or mitigate the fierceness and cruelty of life in its natural state, is weakness and folly and will lead the human race to self-destruction. Man should cease to love himself and his kind and love God in things; he should live outwardly, not inwardly. It is man's turning inward upon himself that Jeffers represents by incest. It follows that Jeffers scorns a life of security and welcomes a life of struggle, pain, and endurance. The qualities he admires are of two kinds: those of the hawk, which represents pride and power, and those of the rock, which represents endurance and final escape from struggle.

His thoughts are best explained in his own language. I quote typical passages from the shorter poems. In "Hooded Night" he says that the stones, the ocean, the cypresses are reality, whereas the whole of man's life and work is "a spectral episode," which will soon be gone and hardly leave a trace in the dark glory of the physical universe. In "The Cruel Falcon" he says:

> *In pleasant peace and security*
> *How suddenly the soul in a man begins to die.*
> *He shall look up above the stalled oxen*
> *Envying the cruel falcon,*
> *And dig under the straw for a stone*
> *To bruise himself on.*

In "Praise Life" he warns us that we cannot banish suffering.

> *Praise life, it deserves praise, but the praise*
> *of life*

> *That forgets the pain is a pebble*
> *Rattled in a dry gourd.*

For American lovers of freedom he has in "Shine, Republic" a stern warning, reminding them that the love of freedom has been the characteristic quality of Western man:

> *And you, America, that passion made you. You were not*
> *born to prosperity, you were born to love freedom.*
> *You did not say "en masse," you said "independence."*
> *But we cannot have all the luxuries and freedom*
> *also.*

> *Freedom is poor and laborious; that torch is not safe but*
> *hungry, and often requires blood for its fuel.*
> *You will tame it against it burn too clearly, you will hood*
> *it like a kept hawk, you will perch it on the wrist*
> *of Caesar.*

> *But keep the tradition, conserve the forms, the observ-*
> *ances, keep the spot sore. Be great, carve deep*
> *your heel-marks.*

> *The states of the next age will no doubt remember you,*
> *and edge their love of freedom with contempt of*
> *luxury.*

In "Signpost" he offers this advice to all men:

> *Turn outward, love things, not men, turn right away*
> *from humanity,*
> *Let that doll lie. Consider if you like how the lilies grow,*
> *Lean on the silent rock until you feel its divinity*

Make your veins cold, look at the silent stars,
    let your eyes
Climb the great ladder out of the pit of yourself and man.
Things are so beautiful, your love will follow your eyes;
Things are the God, you will love God, and not in vain,
For what we love, we grow to it, we share its nature.

And again in "The Answer":

    Integrity is wholeness, the greatest beauty is
Organic wholeness, the wholeness of life and things, the
    divine beauty of the universe. Love that, not man
Apart from that, or else you will share man's pitiful
    confusions, or drown in despair when his days
    darken.

These passages reveal the heart of Jeffers' philosophy. Man should love freedom more than security; he cannot have both. He must accept pain as the price of freedom. Humanity is but a part of nature, and the part is ugly except as it is seen in relation to the whole. The whole is beautiful; it is God. Therefore man must live outwardly and lose his human separateness in the life of the whole. In his conception of the unity of man and nature Jeffers agrees with Emerson and Whitman, but in his rejection of social values (what Whitman called "en masse") he disagrees with them fundamentally. Though loving material nature, Emerson held that spirit and not the fated law of nature is supreme. Whitman assumed spirit and matter to be equal aspects of one entity. Robinson, Frost, and Sandburg, with some differences among them, agree that spirit will eventually become dominant. Jeffers conceives matter as the sole reality, as God, and rejects spirit as a delusion of the human consciousness.

It is clear, then, that Jeffers is not a friend to American idealism. On the contrary, he is definitely opposed to it. Yet his opposition is salutary. We Americans are in danger of yielding to the love of security and luxury and forgetting freedom and pain—or rather we were before the present war. Jeffers warns us that weakness breeds decay and invites destruction. We shall be wise to heed his warning. Though he rejects idealism, his strong love of freedom is the rock on which all idealism must rest. If the truth were known, Jeffers might prove to be more friendly to idealism than he seems. He fears and distrusts the tender quality in idealism, and to offset it he exaggerates the opposite quality of hardness. It will not do to accept Jeffers without condition, but we cannot afford to reject his stern warning that freedom is neither won nor kept without pain.

XI

Retrospects and Prospects

OF THE FORCES THAT HAVE helped to shape the course of American life and literature, two have been predominant: religion and nature. The religion which the first New England settlers brought with them ready made from England, being severely plain and unworldly, found a congenial home in the wilderness. In all ages men have learned that if they would hear the voice of God and stand in his very presence they must seek him in the wilderness. For Puritans, Quakers, and nonconformists of all sects, religion was a personal relation between the individual and God, and when they had exchanged the institutional order of the old world for the primitive freedom of the new, this relationship seemed to them closer than ever before. Their dependence upon the providence of God and their need for community of effort in their struggle against a harsh environment wrought them to such unity in faith and doctrine that they were able to withstand the currents of eighteenth-century skepticism long after it had triumphed in Europe.

The Puritans fostered education, but the schools were controlled by orthodox ministers who did not encourage free speculation in religion. There were always a few communities where one might worship as he pleased, but in any case he was expected to make religious worship in some form a part of his daily life. There was no tolerance anywhere for impiety or infidelity. Liberal ideas were gradually accepted in New England, but deism was never popular. Rationalism in religion, even among the more intellectual classes, usually assumed the mild form of Unitarianism.

In the middle region and to the south neither theology nor piety was as severe as in New England. Distances between settlements were great and schools were rare. Before the Revolution many people felt closer to the mother country than they did to the neighboring colonies. Those who could afford the luxury sent their sons to be educated in England, and these young men often returned with enthusiasm for the deism and humanism that had already become widespread in France and England. The time was ripe for free thinking, and liberals like Benjamin Franklin and Philip Freneau in the middle colonies and Thomas Jefferson in Virginia found many of their neighbors ready to listen to them and to agree with their unorthodox opinions.

When the ferment of romanticism began to work in America, the people of the South looked to Scott and Byron for their models, whereas the people of New England looked rather to Coleridge, Wordsworth, and Carlyle. This was one reason why transcendentalism was widely accepted in New England but not in the South. Through Coleridge and Carlyle, and by other means as well, the New Englanders came under the influence of the German romantic philosophers, while the more realistic Southerners generally followed Locke and the French rationalists. This is a generalization which should not be pressed too far, however; for it must be remembered that Whitman, a New Yorker, was an avowed disciple of Emerson and that Poe, a Virginian, owed much to Coleridge and, in spite of his protestations to the contrary, was strongly transcendental in his thinking.

Whatever foreign influences may have gone into the making of transcendentalism—and they were oriental as well as European—it was primarily a native American product, for it grew out of the fusion of two fundamental American qualities: religious mysticism and the love of nature. The spiritual hunger of the typical American is insatiable, for though he may reach out through newspapers, books, and the theater to possess all experience, he is never satisfied. His desire to possess the material universe is no less powerful, and has made him the most passionate money maker, collector, and traveler the world has ever known. Having pushed his frontier on this continent from the Atlantic to the shores of the Pacific so that he has no more frontiers of his own to develop, he has now for nearly two generations scouted the far places of the globe in search of other means to satisfy his pioneering instinct. It seems to be his destiny to have a hand in the affairs of the whole world despite a traditional policy of isolation. It is not a mere coincidence that New England transcendentalism and Jacksonian democracy belong to the same period in American history. One was a hunger of the soul, the other a hunger of the body, and they were the complementary elements in the new American character. Then, more than in 1776 or 1787, the direction of our cultural development was settled.

This is not to say that either transcendentalism or Jacksonian democracy is to be preserved or revived in its original form. In one movement America found the path leading to its spiritual ideals, and in the other it found the path leading to its political and social ideals; but the paths merely indicate the directions in which we are to travel, not the ends to be sought. One is nature, or the material world; the other is religion, or the life of the soul. The union of the two in literature is proclaimed and exemplified in the poetry of Walt Whitman.

Yet both transcendentalism and democracy began to decline within the lifetimes of Whitman and Emerson. The causes of this decline were numerous and complicated, but they were all symptoms of the unbalanced condition of American life after the Civil War. In Puritan times the life of the spirit had been emphasized to the neglect of the life of the body; now the positions were reversed, and the life of the body was emphasized to the neglect of the spirit. The balance between nature and religion that had been established in the first half of the nineteenth century had been upset. Life on the frontier had necessarily raised material values above spiritual values, and when the frontier expanded more rapidly than it could be absorbed by the older, established communities, its lawless spirit infected the entire country. Religion was not, of course, unknown on the frontier; but it was an unsteady force, tending to burst out at intervals in emotional orgies and then lapse into disuse.

In colonial days, and thereafter in all the newer communities, the individual pioneer had to be ingenious in mechanics in order to survive and maintain his family. This necessity developed in the American people not only an extraordinary aptitude for practical science, but an inordinate enthusiasm for it. By the middle of the last century we had got well started in the work of exploiting the vast natural resources of the country and turning the riches thus amassed into material comforts and luxuries. The nation's appetite grew by what it fed on, with the result that it served the body so completely for six days out of the week that the service of the spirit on Sunday became either a mere interval of relaxation or an emotional purgation in the manner of the frontier revivals. We became a nation of laborers and businessmen who, when we were not at work, demanded sensational pleasures to distract our minds; but the more sensational our pleasures became, the less genuine satisfaction we got out of them.

Inevitably we discovered that our theoretical science had lagged behind our technical science, and that while our outward lives had advanced to the Machine Age, our inward lives followed leisurely at a horse and buggy pace. Outside the universities, where departments of science had grown up and were staffed by professors educated in Germany, there was little interest in science except as it provided people with the conveniences necessary to their new way of life. When Darwin's theories of evolution were made known in this country, the clergy and all the powers of the churches opposed them with great force. Those whose interest it was to maintain the churches and the orthodox creeds as established saw in theoretical science, though not in practical science, their natural enemy. The consequence of the rapid spread of Darwinism and other modern scientific theories among the intellectual classes was a division of the people into two groups, one group clinging to the old creeds and shutting their minds to scientific ideas, the other eagerly devouring the new theories, sometimes without discrimination, and growing more and more antagonistic to church dogmas.

It might be expected that philosophy would bridge the chasm between religion and nature, but there were no philosophers of importance, apart from literature and theology, until near the end of the nineteenth century. Until then the dominant philosophy of the academic philosophers was a modification of German idealism in which the individualism that had been so important an element in transcendentalism was not recognized. Later Royce and Howison made an effort to adapt idealism to American conditions, but their influence did not extend beyond academic circles and a few poets. Far more influential in the country at large were the pragmatists William James and John Dewey. James, sometimes called a neo-transcendentalist though he had no use for the monistic element in transcendentalism, evolved a philosophy of individualism which proved very acceptable to business men and politicians, who found in it a justification of their own methods, however unscrupulous. The pragmatism of Dewey, usually distinguished as instrumentalism, differs from that of James in making social rather than individual welfare the measure of value. James, moreover, was friendly to all forms of religion and himself something of a mystic, whereas Dewey adopted the method of science and appeared to subordinate spiritual to material values. In spite of James's leaning towards transcendentalism, therefore, the pragmatists failed to bridge the gap between religion and nature because their emphasis, on the whole, was too much upon nature and not enough upon religion.

American literature, having its origins in theology and religion, has always been a medium for philosophical speculation. For the poets of the nineteenth century, phi-

losophy has been a link between religion and nature. This
is true not only in the case of transcendentalists like Emerson and Whitman, but also in many other cases. Poe, for
example, attempted in *Eureka* to explain the universe by
combining the methods of empirical science, rational philosophy, and intuitive religion. These poets, as well as
Whittier, Holmes, Longfellow, and Lowell, never fully
accepted the Darwinian theory of evolution, and most of
their poetry was published before this theory had been
generally accepted even by scientists in America. Longfellow's friend Agassiz, for one, never accepted it. Lanier,
however, was sufficiently impressed with the probability
of its truth to be greatly troubled by its antireligious implications. But all the romantic poets from Emerson to
Lanier viewed nature in a religious mood and never
thought of it realistically as the scene of the evolutionary
struggle. Conversely, they freed religion of theological
dogma by restating it in terms of natural benevolence and
natural beauty. Like most other people, they thought of
science as a method by which man is provided with the
means to a more comfortable way of life, and it did not
occur to them that philosophy was involved. Nineteenth
century American poetry, therefore, is predominantly
idealistic and optimistic.

The history of fiction during the same period is very
different. In poetry philosophical ideas may be expressed
directly, but in the novel they are better presented indirectly through action. Being in its nature more closely related to everyday life than poetry and appealing as it does
to the popular taste, the novel reflects the real more than
the ideal, and the scientific attitude towards nature more
than the religious attitude. In this connection it may

be remarked that Hawthorne's treatment of sin is in method and purpose psychological rather than philosophical. Melville is more nearly the philosopher, but it can hardly be supposed that his philosophizing improved his books as novels, however it may have increased their value as books. Except for the homespun moralizing of such characters as Leatherstocking, Cooper introduces no philosophy in his novels, his concern being to solve the problems, individual or social, that confront his characters in specific situations. Already the American novel, even that of Cooper, revealed a mildly pessimistic strain, and this strain deepened as the century drew to an end. The Darwinian theory of evolution undoubtedly was the chief cause of this increasing pessimism. It is a singular fact that novelists have consistently drawn pessimistic conclusions from Darwinism, whereas scientists and philosophers have seen nothing in it to darken the prospect of human life. The general consequences to fiction may be observed in a steady decline from the optimistic realism of Howells to the pessimistic naturalism of Dreiser. In the twentieth century, notwithstanding a few notable exceptions like Willa Cather and Thomas Wolfe, the novelists whose literary reputations are greatest have been naturalists in their method and pessimists in their mood.

The darkening cloud finally cast its shadow upon the poets. Robinson looked without flinching at the unlovely features of reality unveiled by modern science, and though the prospect saddened him it did not embitter his spirit. Frost, too, accepted the conclusions of science, and with a more cheerful countenance. These two acknowledged no inconsistency in a world made up of both spiritual and material values that lead to ends harmoniously conjoined. Sandburg, likewise, although he was more hopeful of the social group than of the individual, maintained his faith in humanity and affirmed a qualified optimism. But the younger poets, those who were born after 1885, could not withstand the double impact of science and the World War, resigned the world to spiritual decay, and followed T. S. Eliot into the waste land of cynicism and defeat.

The drama, too, which had contributed comparatively little to literature in the nineteenth century, now put forth its sickly blossoms in an atmosphere of general decay. Eugene O'Neill, our most distinguished dramatic writer, devotes the resources of his genius to filling the stage with perverted characters that reveal the worst that is in human nature and leave us emotionally unsatisfied and spiritually depressed. In some of his minor works, such as *Ah, Wilderness!*, *Lazarus Laughed,* and *Days Without End,* he leads us to believe that he still retains some faith in the ideals that man has lived by in times past, but the dominant note in his work as a whole is one of inexorable fatalism. Among other contemporary playwrights only Maxwell Anderson and Robert Sherwood need be considered here. Anderson shows sympathy with the basic American idealisms in his poetic drama *Winterset* and in *Candle in the Wind.* Sherwood directly associates himself with the idealists in *Abe Lincoln in Illinois* and in *There Shall Be No Night,* and the popularity of these plays may be an indication that the reign of pessimism in the theater is at an end. But with these exceptions recent dramatists have joined with the novelists and the younger poets in a general chorus of despair.

Idealism was at its lowest ebb and pessimism at full

tide in the decade from 1920 to 1930. The decline of idealism was checked during the economic depression, and now a movement for recovery has set in, though it is painfully slow and not certain to continue. There is ground for hope in the historical fact that the American people have always been optimistic and idealistic by temperament. In fact, it may be doubted whether the pessimism and cynicism so prevalent in recent literature is shared fully by the people as a whole. The class of people that have been most affected are the literary intellectuals, who are perhaps more sensitive to depressive influences than others. The frankest and most alarming statement of this mood was made by Joseph Wood Krutch in *The Modern Temper* (1929), a book which created a sensation when first published. The world of modern science, says Mr. Krutch, is one in which the intellect rejoices, but the spirit, deprived of the illusions upon which it lives, shrivels and dies. He assumes that the universe is wholly material and that the spiritual world which mankind in past times has believed to be real was only an illusion. An intelligent man, he thinks, can no longer believe in the reality of his own soul. Man, therefore, is confronted with the terrible dilemma: he must cease to exist altogether and leave the earth to soulless beings or himself become soulless; for all his spiritual values are predicated on a world that never existed except in his deluded imagination and can no longer exist even there. Krutch sees evidence already that man is abandoning his human characteristics, which are incongruous in the universe that science has revealed to him, and reverting rapidly to his purely animal nature. He is not himself willing to take this course, and therefore he is reconciled to increasing unhappiness and eventual annihilation. Thus Mr. Krutch, whom I take to be a disillusioned idealist.

But surely our future is not so dark as it is painted in *The Modern Temper*. Perhaps Mr. Krutch and his temperamental friends were merely suffering from a bad case of the jitters. The man in the street is more hopeful, and the philosophers seem unperturbed. T. V. Smith, a contemporary pragmatist, acknowledges his belief that all things are material in their origin, even the poet's imagination and the idealist's dream of absolute truth. But he is concerned less about what things come from and more about what they lead to; and he is willing, for the present at least, to consign spirit to the realm of imagination rather than to the realm of truth. So long as spiritual values function as if they were true they have meaning, and he finds meaning a more profitable study for the philosopher than truth. Mr. Smith is a bold materialist. The soul, he affirms, develops from the material organism and is a social product. In this fact, however, he finds ground for hope rather than despair, for if the soul originates in matter and is shaped by human conditions, it should be as much at home in the scientist's material universe as any other purely animal being.

Smith's realm of imagination is surprisingly like the world of illusions which Robinson describes in *Amaranth*, a world in which the earnest truth seeker cannot abide. But in justice to the philosopher it must be added that his realm of imagination is not the negation of truth; in some ways he thinks it is *beyond* truth, or what traditional philosophers have taken for truth, and that having explored meaning the seeker may be given a new insight that will make the search for truth more fruitful than it has been heretofore. There are two significant and comforting affirmations in the philosophy of T. V. Smith. One is an affirmation that spiritual values, though they must somehow evolve from matter, are true for us because they function as if they were true. The other is an affirmation that the social medium which gives meaning to man as a spiritual being makes democracy possible and desirable. There is in all this a decided Whitmanian flavor. It would perhaps be fair to say that T. V. Smith, like a good many of his colleagues, is a materialist in his ontology but an idealist in his social philosophy.

Even the philosophers themselves admit that it is hard to distinguish the materialists, realists, and the idealists among their contemporaries from one another. Sidney Hook says that "if and when" there is a conflict between materialism and idealism it is a conflict between naturalism and supernaturalism, and he concludes that such a conflict cannot be resolved by the methods of philosophy. Moreover, he sees no connection between the political or social belief that a man holds and his classification as materialist or idealist. He himself, I believe, is a Marxist or is inclined in that direction. In the present study I have assumed generally that an idealist is one who believes that the ultimate reality is spiritual and that the universe is purposive in its evolution. I have supposed that a materialist is one who denies both the spiritual character of reality and the purposive character of evolution. But this distinction is hard to maintain at the present time. Santayana, who called himself a materialist, admitted that it is only for the sake of the free life of the spirit that the material world is worth knowing and possessing. Professor Woodbridge, also a materialist, affirmed that nature is teleological, not in a general drift towards some common result, but in special cases; and that consciousness, which is such a special case, involves moral responsibility and the obligation on the part of man to believe in the possibility of moral progress. Thus he concluded, on the basis of natural teleology, that ours is the best possible world because it has the capacity to engender and support the effort to make it better.

On the other hand, W. E. Hocking, who is one of the relatively few avowed idealists among contemporary American philosophers, agrees that the real, the One, cannot be finally known; but he believes that seeking implies some degree of finding, else life for a rational being would be a mockery, and that the mind advances from one partial success to another in the direction of knowledge of the real and is encouraged by this progress to continue its effort. A. N. Whitehead, who may perhaps without impropriety be included among American philosophers, does not classify himself, but some idealists claim him as one of their group. He sometimes uses the terms "feeling" and "experience" in place of "mind," and seems to attribute mind thus defined to plants and inorganic objects as well as to animals. This places him very near the position of the materialists who derive mind from matter. There is, in short, a tendency among philosophers, and the same may be said with some qualification of scientists, to break down the distinction between mind and matter, not, as in the past, by calling one real and the other apparent, but by considering them both real and in their ultimate nature one identical substance.

This new idealism of Whitehead has much in common with Emerson's theory of a polarized universe and still more with Whitman's theory that spirit and matter are complementary functions of a unitary reality. This similarity may be partly explained by the fact that there have been two cycles in the development of American idealism, the first cycle culminating in transcendentalism and the second not yet at the end of its culminating movement. This cyclic pattern is produced by the shifting of emphasis from religion to its polar opposite, nature, and the subsequent harmonizing of the two. In the beginning religion was the more important, yet both religion and nature were held together by the supernatural authority of a personal deity. In the eighteenth century, skepticism undermined this authority and prepared the way for the substitution of reason for supernatural authority. This weakened the force of religion and allowed nature to rise to the dominant position. In the first half of the nineteenth century the two were harmonized in transcendentalism, which united matter (the substance in nature) and spirit (the agent in religion) in the individual organism. The social counterpart of transcendentalism was the individualism of Jacksonian democracy.

But nature continued to grow in importance until the balance was again upset, beginning the second cyclic movement. Darwin's theory of evolution by natural selection undermined the spiritual basis of transcendentalism and precipitated a wave of skepticism and pessimism. At the same time, the frontier spirit, which had been a wholesome element in building Jacksonian democracy, led to social chaos in the Machine Age. Pragmatism in philosophy was an effort to give direction to the materialism of American life, but it was claimed by many Americans as a justification of laissez-faire capitalism. In recent years,

however, both scientists and philosophers have been active
in preparing a new interpretation of nature which may restore it to a state of harmony with religion. When this last
movement in the second cycle shall have been completed,
we may expect a renaissance of the spirit accompanied by
achievements in literature as great as those of the nineteenth century or even greater. We may expect corresponding achievements in economics and statecraft. Obviously it is impossible to foretell what these new achievements will be like, but I believe there is ground for hope
that they will be democratic and idealistic in their nature
and that they will be a great benefit to the world in
general.

In the eighteenth century it seemed to many that
rationalism and the frontier were subversive forces in
American life, but we know now that they were active
agents in the creation of the new stability of the nineteenth
century. Similarly, it seemed to many in the late nineteenth and early twentieth centuries that science and materialism were subversive forces. Although it is too early
to know what these two forces will finally contribute to
our civilization, we can be reasonably sure that they will
not alter its fundamental character. That character, as
we have seen, depends upon a harmonious relationship
between religion and nature as main determinants of
American philosophy, which, with all our pragmatic materialism, has been dominantly idealistic from the beginning. The same forces that pulled down the old idealism
promise to raise up the new, and so it must always be; for
idealism is not a theory or a fact which the mind possesses,
but a quality of the mind itself.

Index

Index   **229**

Index

American Idealism

HAS BEEN SET IN THE TWELVE POINT SIZE

OF LINOTYPE CASLON OLD FACE

AND PRINTED UPON

WOVE ANTIQUE

PAPER

UNIVERSITY OF OKLAHOMA PRESS

NORMAN